Northern Italy Tour Book 2023

Unveiling Northern Italy: Discover Venice, Milan, Verona, and More | Insider's Guide to History, Art, Food, and Culture

Fosco Manna

All rights reserved. No part of this publication may be reproduced, distributed,or transmitted in any form or by any means, including photocopying, recording, or other electronic or mechanical methods, without the prior written permission of the publisher, except in the case of brief quotations embodied in critical reviews and certain other noncommercial uses permitted by copyright law.

Copyright © Fosco Manna,2023.

Table of contents

Introduction
- Climate and Weather
- Travel Tips and Resources

Chapter 1
Exploring Milan
- Where to Stay
- What to Eat and Where
- Tourist Attractions in Milan
- Things to do in Milan

Chapter 2
Discovering Venice
- Where to Stay
- What to Eat and Where
- Tourist Attractions in Venice
- Things to do in Venice

Chapter 3
Exploring Verona and the Veneto Region
- Where to Stay
- What to Eat and Where

- Tourist Attractions in Verona
- Things to do in Verona

Chapter 4
Turin and the Piedmont Region
- Where to Stay
- What to Eat and Where
- Tourist Attractions in Turin and the Piedmont Region
- Things to do in Turin and the Piedmont Region

Chapter 5
Emilia-Romagna
- Where to Stay
- What to Eat and Where
- Tourist Attractions in Emilia-Romagna
- Things to do in Emilia-Romagna

Chapter 6
Discovering Friuli-Venezia Giulia
- Where to Stay
- What to Eat and Where
- Top Attractions in

Friuli-Venezia Giulia
- Things to do in Friuli-Venezia Giulia

Chapter 7
 Italian Lakes and Alpine Retreats

Chapter 8
 Transportation Options

Chapter 9
 Basic Italian Phrases

Conclusion

Introduction

Welcome to a land of captivating beauty, where ancient history and modern innovation intertwine effortlessly against a backdrop of breathtaking landscapes. Nestled in the northern reaches of Italy, this enchanting region beckons travelers with its rich tapestry of culture, art, gastronomy, and unparalleled charm. From the cosmopolitan allure of **Milan** to the romantic waterways of **Venice**, the majestic peaks of the **Dolomites** to the serene shores of the *Italian Lakes*, Northern Italy is a treasure trove of wonders waiting to be explored.

Northern Italy is a place where the past gracefully mingles with the present, where the whispers of long-forgotten tales can still be heard echoing through cobblestone streets and magnificent piazzas. Each city and region holds a unique story, revealing itself in the intricate details of its architecture, the vibrant hues of its art, and the tantalizing flavors of its cuisine. Prepare to immerse yourself in a world where the passion for design and fashion sets the trends for the world.

Begin your journey in Milan, the pulsating heart of Northern Italy. This vibrant metropolis embodies sophistication and style, where historic landmarks stand tall alongside modern skyscrapers. Lose yourself in the intricate elegance of the Duomo, marvel at masterpieces in world-class galleries, and indulge in a shopping experience that is nothing short of extraordinary. Then venture further, where Venice beckons with its romantic allure. Traverse the shimmering canals aboard a gondola, get lost in its labyrinthine streets, and revel in the beauty of palaces rising from the waters, embracing the eternal spirit of this floating city.

Explore the picturesque towns and rolling vineyards of the Veneto region, savoring the finest wines and culinary delights that grace your palate. Embrace the grandeur of Turin and the Piedmont region, where history and gastronomy harmonize to create an unforgettable experience. And let the tranquility of the Italian Lakes wash over you, as you bask in the serenity of <u>Lake Como, Lake Garda, and Lake Maggiore,</u> surrounded by picturesque towns and breathtaking vistas.

Northern Italy is also a realm of artistic and cultural treasures. Wander through the mosaic-adorned streets of Ravenna, marveling at Byzantine masterpieces. Lose yourself in the gastronomic paradise of Emilia-Romagna, where _Parmigiano-Reggiano cheese_, _balsamic vinegar,_ and mouthwatering _cured meats_ take center stage. Finally, uncover the hidden gems of Friuli-Venezia Giulia, where the Adriatic Sea kisses the rugged Carso Plateau, and where a fusion of cultures creates a vibrant and unique atmosphere.

This **Northern Italy travel guide** is your key to unlocking the secrets of this extraordinary region. Delve into its chapters, and let yourself be transported on a captivating journey through time and space. Whether you seek artistic inspiration, culinary delights, natural wonders, or simply the joy of exploration, Northern Italy awaits with open arms, ready to leave an indelible mark on your heart and soul. Get ready to embark on an unforgettable adventure through the timeless charm of Northern Italy.

Climate and Weather

When it comes to the climate and weather, Northern Italy holds a delightful surprise for every season. Nature's brush strokes paint a vibrant picture, creating a tapestry of changing landscapes that captivate the senses throughout the year.

In the spring, the region awakens from its winter slumber, offering a spectacle of blooming flowers and budding trees. The air is crisp, carrying with it a gentle warmth that entices you to explore the lush gardens and parks that come to life. As the days grow longer, the countryside transforms into a kaleidoscope of vibrant colors, beckoning you to wander through rolling hills and vineyards, and indulge in the sweet scent of blossoms.

Summer arrives, bringing with it a sun-drenched embrace that bathes Northern Italy in warmth and radiance. The days are filled with sunshine and blue skies, creating the perfect backdrop for leisurely strolls along cobblestone streets or relaxing moments by the shimmering lakes. As temperatures rise, coastal towns and beaches become a haven for those seeking refreshing dips in the azure waters of the Adriatic or Mediterranean Sea. It's a time to savor gelato under the shade of ancient monuments and to revel in the lively outdoor festivals that fill the air with music and laughter.

Autumn unveils its majestic palette, as the landscape transforms into a symphony of fiery reds, oranges, and yellows. The air carries a crispness, inviting you to wrap yourself in a cozy sweater and embark on scenic hikes through the awe-inspiring Dolomites or the picturesque trails that wind through national parks. It's a season of harvest, where vineyards come alive with the bustling activity of grape-pickers, and the aroma of freshly pressed olive oil permeates the air. Fall is the perfect time to savor the region's renowned culinary delights, as truffles, porcini mushrooms, and hearty stews grace the tables of welcoming trattorias.

Winter casts its enchantment over Northern Italy, transforming the landscape into a winter wonderland. Snow-capped peaks of the Alps and Dolomites beckon ski enthusiasts to carve their way down pristine slopes. Christmas markets fill town squares, offering a magical ambiance with twinkling lights, handcrafted ornaments, and the scent of mulled wine and roasted chestnuts. Cozy up beside a crackling fireplace in a charming mountain chalet, or venture into the cities, where theaters come alive with performances and museums offer respite from the chill.

As you embark on your journey through Northern Italy, remember to embrace the ever-changing climate and weather that add a touch of magic to your experiences. Whether you find yourself basking in the warm embrace of summer, marveling at the vibrant colors of autumn, or wrapped in a winter's embrace, Northern Italy offers a climate that enhances every aspect of your travel adventure. So pack your suitcase with layers and anticipation, and let nature's gift unveil itself as you immerse yourself in the captivating beauty of this remarkable region.

Travel Tips and Resources

Embarking on a voyage to Northern Italy is an opportunity to embrace new experiences, immerse yourself in captivating culture, and create lifelong memories. To ensure your journey is smooth and unforgettable, here are some essential travel tips to consider:

1. Embrace the Art of Slow Travel:
Northern Italy is a region best savored at a leisurely pace. Give yourself the time to wander aimlessly through narrow streets, sit at sidewalk cafes, and soak up the ambiance. Embrace the Italian concept of (the sweetness of doing nothing) and savor every moment.

2. Connect with the Local Culture:
Engage with the locals and immerse yourself in the vibrant Italian culture. Learn a few basic Italian phrases and greet people with a warm smile. Don't be afraid to strike up conversations with shopkeepers, baristas, or fellow travelers. It's through these interactions that you'll truly uncover the essence of Northern Italy.

3. Explore Beyond the Tourist Hotspots:
While iconic cities like Milan and Venice are must-visit destinations, venture off the beaten path to discover hidden gems. Explore lesser-known towns, charming countryside, and picturesque coastal villages. These off-the-radar places often offer authentic experiences and a chance to connect with the local way of life.

4. Indulge in Culinary Delights:

Northern Italy is a culinary paradise, so be sure to indulge in the region's gastronomic treasures. Sample fresh pasta, melt-in-your-mouth gelato, and exquisite regional wines. Seek out local trattorias and family-run restaurants for an authentic taste of Italian cuisine. Don't forget to try the regional specialties like risotto in Milan or balsamic vinegar in Modena.

5. Get Lost in Time:
Let yourself wander without a fixed itinerary. Explore hidden alleys, stumble upon tucked-away squares, and get lost in the labyrinthine streets of ancient cities. Serendipitous discoveries await at every turn, whether it's stumbling upon a charming artisan shop or stumbling upon a hidden viewpoint with breathtaking vistas.

6. Embrace the Artistic Heritage:

Northern Italy is a haven for art enthusiasts. Immerse yourself in the masterpieces of renowned artists like da Vinci, Michelangelo, and Caravaggio. Visit world-class museums, galleries, and churches to witness the timeless beauty of Italian art and architecture. Be sure to book tickets in advance for popular attractions to avoid long queues.

7. Pack Smart and Travel Light:

Packing light is the key to stress-free travel. Check the weather forecast for your travel period and pack versatile clothing suitable for layering. Comfortable walking shoes are a must, as exploring Northern Italy often involves walking on cobblestone streets and uneven terrain. Consider a compact day bag for essentials during your daily explorations.

8. <u>Stay Flexible and Open</u>:

Embrace the unexpected and allow room for spontaneity. It's in the unexpected detours and unplanned moments that the most magical experiences often unfold. Embrace the Italian concept of (the sweet life) and savor each twist and turn of your journey.

Remember, traveling to Northern Italy is about creating cherished memories and connecting with the heart and soul of this remarkable region. Soak in the beauty, flavors, and warmth of the Italian way of life, and let your journey unfold with the spirit of adventure. Bon viaggio!

Chapter 1

Exploring Milan

Milan is located in the heart of Northern Italy, Milan stands as a vibrant metropolis that seamlessly blends history, innovation, and an undeniable sense of style. As the region's cosmopolitan capital, Milan offers a captivating tapestry of experiences that captivate travelers from around the world.

Renowned as a global fashion and design hub, Milan sets the trends that shape the industry. The city's elegant streets and high-end boutiques beckon fashion enthusiasts, while the annual _Milan Fashion Week_ showcases the latest creations of renowned designers. From the luxury of Via Montenapoleone to the trendy Navigli district, Milan's fashion scene reflects its innate sense of style and refinement.

Beyond its fashion prowess, Milan is a treasure trove of cultural and artistic wonders. The awe-inspiring **Duomo**, with its intricately carved facade and breathtaking views from the rooftop, stands as an iconic symbol of the city's grandeur. Just steps away, the **Galleria Vittorio Emanuele II** invites visitors to wander through its opulent halls, housing luxury shops, historic cafes, and a true architectural masterpiece.

Art enthusiasts can revel in Milan's rich artistic heritage. The renowned _Pinacoteca di Brera_ houses an impressive collection of Italian Renaissance masterpieces, while Leonardo's magnum opus, "<u>The Last Supper,</u>" can be admired at the Convent of Santa Maria delle Grazie, a testament to Milan's connection to artistic genius.

As day turns into night, Milan comes alive with its vibrant nightlife and gastronomic delights. Savor traditional Milanese cuisine, characterized by delicate flavors and the use of high-quality ingredients. From the cozy trattorias serving creamy risotto alla milanese to trendy Michelin-starred restaurants pushing culinary boundaries, Milan's dining scene satisfies even the most discerning palate.

Milan is not just about the glitz and glamour. It's a city of contrasts, where ancient history and modern innovation coexist harmoniously. The sleek skyscrapers of the <u>Porta Nuova</u> district stand in contrast to the centuries-old

Sforza Castle, which houses impressive art collections and tranquil gardens. The futuristic and environmentally sustainable Vertical Forest, with its verdant facade, reflects Milan's commitment to architectural innovation and sustainability.

Milan's spirit extends beyond its borders, inviting visitors to explore the surrounding Lombardy region. Discover the enchanting beauty of **Lake Como**, with its sparkling waters framed by majestic mountains and elegant villas. Immerse yourself in the artistic heritage of Bergamo's Città Alta, a medieval gem with cobblestone streets and ancient walls. And for motorsport enthusiasts, a pilgrimage to Monza's legendary racetrack is a must, where the roar of engines and the adrenaline of speed fill the air.

Milan embodies the essence of Northern Italy—a region that effortlessly marries tradition and innovation, history and contemporary flair. It invites travelers to uncover its secrets, embrace its unparalleled style, and immerse themselves in a city where creativity and cultural richness thrive. So come, be captivated by the timeless allure of Milan, and allow yourself to be swept away by its undeniable charm.

Where to Stay

When it comes to finding the ideal place to stay in Milan, the city offers a wide range of options to suit every traveler's preferences and budget. Whether you seek luxurious elegance, boutique charm, or budget-friendly comfort, Milan has a plethora of accommodations that will ensure a memorable stay. Here are some recommendations to help you find your perfect home away from home:

1. **Historic Elegance**

Immerse yourself in the grandeur of Milan's history by staying in one of the city's historic hotels. These opulent establishments have witnessed centuries of charm and offer exquisite accommodations coupled with impeccable service. From the iconic **Hotel Principe di Savoia** to the elegant **Palazzo Parigi Hotel & Grand Spa,** these properties blend classic luxury with modern amenities.

2. **Chic Boutique**

For those seeking a more intimate and personalized experience, Milan boasts a wealth of boutique hotels that exude style and sophistication. These hidden gems offer unique design, artistic touches, and attentive service. Consider the **Bulgari Hotel Milano,** blending contemporary elegance with Italian craftsmanship, or the **Magna Pars Suites Milano**, a former perfume factory transformed into a stylish oasis.

3. City Center Convenience

To fully immerse yourself in the energy of Milan's city center, choose accommodations in the heart of the action. Staying near the *Piazza del Duomo* or the *Brera district* puts you within walking distance of iconic landmarks, designer boutiques, and trendy restaurants. The luxury **Hotel Milano Scala** or the contemporary **Room Mate Giulia** are excellent options in central locations.

4. Trendy Navigli District

For a more bohemian and artistic vibe, consider the vibrant Navigli district. This canal-lined neighborhood is renowned for its trendy bars, lively nightlife, and charming atmosphere. Stay in one of the boutique hotels in the area, such as the art-inspired **_Yard Milano_** or the contemporary **_Maison Borella_**, and immerse yourself in the local creative scene.

5. Fashionable Quadrilatero della Moda

Fashion enthusiasts can opt for accommodations in the Quadrilatero della Moda, the famous fashion district. This upscale area is home to renowned designer boutiques and high-end shopping streets like Via Montenapoleone and Via della Spiga. Treat yourself to the luxurious **_Bulgari Milano_** or the sophisticated **_Armani Hotel Milano_**, both situated in this fashionable neighborhood.

6. Budget-Friendly Options

Milan also offers a range of budget-friendly accommodations without compromising on comfort or convenience. From cozy bed and breakfasts to well-appointed guesthouses, there are options to suit different budgets. **The Zebra Hostel** and **Hotel Berna** are popular choices that provide affordable comfort and proximity to transportation hubs.

7. Airbnb and Apartment Rentals

For a more home-like experience, consider renting an apartment or booking a room through Airbnb. This option allows you to live like a local, offering more space and the opportunity to explore Milan from a residential neighborhood. From modern lofts to traditional apartments, there's a wide variety of choices to suit your needs.

When choosing where to stay in Milan, consider factors such as location, amenities, and personal preferences. Remember to book in advance, especially during peak travel seasons, to secure your preferred accommodation. Whether you seek luxury, boutique charm, or budget-friendly comfort, Milan's diverse range of accommodations ensures that your stay in this remarkable city will be nothing short of exceptional.

What to Eat and Where

Milan is not only a fashion and design capital but also a haven for food enthusiasts eager to indulge in the delectable flavors of Northern Italian cuisine. From traditional Milanese dishes to international culinary delights, the city offers a diverse dining scene that caters to every palate. Here are some culinary recommendations and where to find them:

1. Risotto alla Milanese at Trattoria Milanese

Begin your culinary journey in Milan with the iconic dish of the city, *Risotto alla Milanese*. This creamy saffron-infused rice dish is a true gastronomic delight. Head to Trattoria Milanese, a historic establishment dating back to 1933, to savor their renowned risotto prepared to perfection. The restaurant's warm ambiance and traditional Milanese recipes make it an ideal spot for an authentic dining experience.

2. Cotoletta alla Milanese at Osteria della Vite

For a true taste of Milanese tradition, indulge in Cotoletta alla Milanese, a breaded and fried veal cutlet that is crispy on the outside and tender on the inside. Osteria della Vite, located near the Brera district, serves a mouthwatering version of this classic dish. Accompanied by a side of golden fries or a refreshing salad, this hearty meal is a must-try.

3. Aperitivo at Navigli District

Experience the beloved Milanese tradition of aperitivo, an early evening ritual of enjoying drinks accompanied by a variety of appetizers. Head to the lively Navigli district, where you'll find a plethora of bars and restaurants offering enticing aperitivo spreads. Grab a seat at Al Pont de Ferr, where you can savor a refreshing cocktail while enjoying an array of delectable nibbles.

4. Panettone at Pasticceria Marchesi

No visit to Milan is complete without savoring a slice of Panettone, the city's iconic Christmas cake. Pasticceria Marchesi, a historic pastry shop established in 1824, is renowned for its exquisite Panettone. Delight in the delicate flavors and soft texture of this traditional sweet treat while sipping a cup of coffee in their elegant tearoom.

5. Seafood at Langosteria

Milan's culinary scene extends beyond traditional dishes to include a variety of international flavors. Langosteria, a renowned seafood restaurant, offers a delightful selection of fresh fish and seafood dishes. Indulge in dishes like raw oysters, seafood pasta, or the catch of the day, expertly prepared to highlight the natural flavors of the ingredients.

6. Gelato at Gelateria della Musica

Treat yourself to the creamy goodness of artisanal gelato at Gelateria della Musica. With a wide range of flavors made from high-quality ingredients, this popular gelateria is a favorite among locals and visitors alike. From classic flavors like pistachio and stracciatella to inventive combinations, such as ricotta and figs or lavender and white peach, you'll find a gelato to tantalize your taste buds.

7. International Cuisine at Eataly

For a culinary adventure that spans various regions of Italy, head to Eataly, a gourmet food emporium located near the Smeraldo Theater. This sprawling marketplace offers a wide array of Italian products, including fresh produce, cured meats, cheeses, and artisanal bread. Explore the different eateries within Eataly to sample dishes from various

Italian regions, from Neapolitan pizza to Sicilian cannoli.

Milan's culinary scene is a testament to its vibrant and diverse culture. Whether you're exploring traditional Milanese dishes, indulging in international flavors, or satisfying your sweet tooth with delightful pastries and gelato, Milan has something to offer for every culinary preference. As you explore the city, be sure to venture beyond the popular tourist areas and seek out local trattorias, osterias, and hidden gems to truly immerse yourself in the authentic Milanese food culture.

Remember, part of the joy of dining in Milan is the ambiance and atmosphere that accompanies the food. Take your time to savor each bite, enjoy the lively conversations around you, and embrace the Milanese tradition of dining as a social experience. Whether you're dining in a cozy neighborhood trattoria or a chic restaurant in the city center, let the flavors of Milan tantalize your taste buds and create unforgettable culinary memories.

Tourist Attractions in Milan

Milan, a city steeped in history, art, and innovation, beckons travelers with its captivating blend of tradition and modernity. From awe-inspiring architectural wonders to world-class museums and vibrant cultural hubs, Milan offers a treasure trove of attractions that leave visitors in awe. Join us on a journey as we unveil the city's most renowned tourist destinations, where each step unveils a new layer of Milan's rich tapestry.

1. Milan Cathedral (Duomo di Milano)

Standing proudly at the heart of the city, the Milan Cathedral, or Duomo di Milano, is a masterpiece of Gothic architecture that commands attention. Its intricate facade, adorned with countless spires, statues, and delicate marble details, is a testament to the city's grandeur. Ascend to the rooftop terraces for panoramic views of Milan and marvel at the impressive marble sculptures that punctuate the roofline.

2. Galleria Vittorio Emanuele II

Adjacent to the Duomo, the Galleria Vittorio Emanuele II is a spectacular 19th-century arcade that epitomizes elegance and luxury. Wander through its soaring iron-and-glass vaulted ceilings, adorned with mosaics and decorative motifs. This architectural gem houses high-end boutiques, historic cafes, and renowned restaurants. Don't forget to spin on the bull's mosaic in the center for good luck!

3. The Last Supper at Santa Maria delle Grazie

An artistic masterpiece that needs no introduction, Leonardo da Vinci's "**The Last Supper**" resides in the refectory of the Convent of Santa Maria delle Grazie. Book your timed entry ticket well in advance to witness this iconic mural, which captures the emotional intensity of the Last Supper. Allow the intricate details and sublime composition to transport you to another era.

4. Sforza Castle (Castello Sforzesco)

Nestled amidst lush gardens, the Sforza Castle stands as a symbol of power and elegance. This imposing fortress once served as the residence of the ruling Sforza dynasty. Explore its extensive courtyards, wander through its museums, and marvel at the exquisite frescoes and sculptures housed within its walls. Don't miss Michelangelo's unfinished masterpiece, the Rondanini Pietà, displayed in the Castle's Museum of Ancient Art.

5. Brera Art Gallery (Pinacoteca di Brera)
Art enthusiasts should not miss the opportunity to visit the Brera Art Gallery, one of Italy's finest art collections. Housed in a former monastery, this museum showcases an exceptional array of Italian Renaissance masterpieces. Admire works by renowned artists such as Raphael, Caravaggio, and Mantegna, as well as lesser-known gems. The gallery's atmospheric setting and refined curation make it a must-visit for art lovers.

6. La Scala Opera House (Teatro alla Scala)

Immerse yourself in the world of opera and classical music by visiting the legendary La Scala Opera House. This renowned theater has witnessed some of the most illustrious performances in history. Take a guided tour to explore the opulent auditorium, adorned with plush velvet seats and gilded decorations. Delve into the theater's rich history, and if you're lucky, secure tickets to a performance for an unforgettable cultural experience.

7. Navigli District

Venture to the charming Navigli district, famous for its picturesque canals and vibrant ambiance. Stroll along the banks of the Naviglio Grande and Naviglio Pavese, lined with colorful buildings, quaint shops, and bustling cafes. This lively neighborhood comes alive in the evening, with numerous bars and restaurants offering a myriad of dining and entertainment options. Indulge in aperitivo at one of the many trendy bars, or dine al fresco at a canal-side restaurant while savoring Milanese delicacies.

8. Leonardo da Vinci National Museum of Science and Technology

Delve into the world of science and innovation at the Leonardo da Vinci National Museum of Science and Technology. This interactive museum pays homage to the genius of Leonardo da Vinci, showcasing his inventions and pioneering contributions across various fields. Explore the exhibits on astronomy, transportation, energy, and more, and witness the replica of da Vinci's famous flying machines.

9. Quadrilatero della Moda (Fashion Quadrilateral)

Embark on a fashion pilgrimage in the Quadrilatero della Moda, Milan's high-end fashion district. Discover the prestigious boutiques of renowned designers and luxury fashion houses, including Via Montenapoleone, Via della Spiga, and Via Sant'Andrea. Admire the latest fashion trends and soak in the glamorous atmosphere of this exclusive shopping destination.

10. San Maurizio al Monastero Maggiore

Hidden behind an unassuming facade lies a hidden gem of Milan's artistic heritage, the San Maurizio al Monastero Maggiore. Step inside this lesser-known church to discover breathtaking frescoes that rival those of the Sistine Chapel. Admire the intricately painted scenes depicting religious narratives, stunning architectural details, and a sense of serenity that envelops this hidden artistic treasure.

11. Piazza del Duomo

Return to the heart of the city and soak in the vibrant atmosphere of Piazza del Duomo. Marvel at the grandeur of the Milan Cathedral, admire the equestrian statue of Vittorio Emanuele II, and take in the architectural splendor of the surrounding buildings. This bustling square serves as a meeting point, a gathering place, and a testament to Milan's rich history and contemporary vitality.

12. Porta Nuova District

Witness the modern face of Milan in the Porta Nuova district, a thriving urban area characterized by sleek skyscrapers, innovative architecture, and urban regeneration. Visit the Vertical Forest (Bosco Verticale), an impressive pair of residential towers covered in greenery, symbolizing the city's commitment to sustainable living. Explore the district's modern art installations, stylish boutiques, and trendy cafes that reflect Milan's forward-thinking spirit.

13. Civic Aquarium of Milan (Acquario Civico di Milano)

Take a journey under the sea at the Civic Aquarium of Milan, one of the oldest aquariums in Europe. Explore the diverse marine life showcased in its tanks and discover fascinating ecosystems from around the world. From colorful tropical fish to majestic sharks, the aquarium offers an immersive experience that delights both young and old.

14. Indulge in Local Cuisine and Markets

No visit to Milan is complete without savoring the city's culinary delights. Explore the local markets, such as Mercato di Porta Romana and Mercato di Via Fauchè, to experience the vibrant food culture of Milan. Sample regional cheeses, cured meats, fresh produce, and artisanal bread. Indulge in traditional Milanese dishes, such as ossobuco (braised veal shanks) or risotto alla milanese (saffron risotto), at authentic trattorias and osterias scattered throughout the city.

15. Corso Como

Escape the bustling city streets and find respite in the trendy neighborhood of Corso Como. This fashionable district is renowned for its stylish boutiques, art galleries, and design stores. Explore concept stores and browse the latest fashion trends, or relax at a chic café while observing the fashionable Milanese crowd. Corso Como perfectly blends art, design, and fashion, making it a haven for creativity and inspiration.

16. Fondazione Prada

Art aficionados should make a beeline for the Fondazione Prada, an art complex that pushes the boundaries of contemporary art and culture. Housed in a former gin distillery, the foundation showcases thought-provoking exhibitions, installations, and performances by renowned international artists. Wander through its galleries, immerse yourself in multimedia installations, and engage in dialogues about the evolving nature of art.

17. Porta Ticinese and the Naviglio Grande

Explore the lively district of Porta Ticinese, known for its bohemian atmosphere and artistic vibe. Take a leisurely stroll along the picturesque Naviglio Grande, lined with charming cafes, vintage shops, and art studios. Enjoy a drink at a waterside bar and savor the vibrant energy of this enchanting neighborhood. On weekends, the area transforms into a bustling antiques market, where you can hunt for unique treasures.

18. Triennale Design Museum
Delve into the world of design at the Triennale Design Museum, a hub dedicated to contemporary design, architecture, and visual arts. This cultural institution hosts exhibitions that showcase innovative design concepts, cutting-edge installations, and thought-provoking displays. Explore the museum's collection, attend design

workshops, and gain insight into the evolving landscape of design.

19. Orto Botanico di Brera

Find tranquility amidst the city's hustle and bustle at the Orto Botanico di Brera, a peaceful botanical garden nestled in the heart of Milan. Wander through its lush greenery, admire the diverse plant species, and discover hidden corners that offer a moment of serenity. This hidden oasis provides a welcome escape from the urban environment and a chance to connect with nature.

20. Fashion and Design Museums

Pay homage to Milan's status as a global fashion and design capital by visiting its renowned museums. Explore the fashion-focused exhibits at the Fashion Museum (Museo della Moda), where you can trace the evolution of Italian fashion through the ages. Alternatively, visit the Design Museum (Museo del Design) to delve into the world of Italian design, from furniture and industrial design to fashion accessories and innovative creations.

21. The Columns of San Lorenzo

Uncover the ancient history of Milan at the Columns of San Lorenzo, a captivating archaeological site located near the Basilica of San Lorenzo. These ancient Roman columns stand as a testament to the city's past, and the surrounding square is a popular gathering place for locals and visitors alike. Enjoy the vibrant atmosphere, sit on the steps, and soak in the ambiance of this historic corner of Milan.

22. Cimitero Monumentale

Venture beyond traditional tourist attractions and visit the Cimitero Monumentale, a stunningly beautiful cemetery that doubles as an open-air museum. Stroll along its winding paths adorned with elaborate sculptures, grand mausoleums, and artistic tombs. This serene and evocative place offers a unique glimpse into Milan's artistic heritage and serves as a final resting place for many prominent figures from history.

As you explore these captivating attractions, allow yourself to be immersed in Milan's unique blend of history, art, and contemporary charm. Each destination offers a glimpse into the city's rich cultural heritage and vibrant present. Whether you're marveling at architectural masterpieces, delving into artistic treasures, or indulging in culinary delights, Milan captivates the senses and leaves an indelible impression on every traveler. The city's allure lies not only in its iconic landmarks but also in its vibrant neighborhoods, charming streets, and the warmth of its people.

Things to do in Milan

1. Visit the Milan Cathedral (Duomo di Milano)

Marvel at the grandeur of one of the world's largest Gothic cathedrals. Explore its intricate details, climb to the rooftop for panoramic views, and immerse yourself in the spiritual ambiance of this iconic landmark.

2. Explore the Galleria Vittorio Emanuele II

Step into this elegant shopping arcade, adorned with beautiful architecture and high-end stores. Indulge in some retail therapy, sip coffee at historic cafes, and admire the stunning glass dome.

3. **Admire Da Vinci's "The Last Supper"**
Book a reservation to see this renowned fresco painting in the refectory of the Convent of Santa Maria delle Grazie. Appreciate the artistic genius of Leonardo da Vinci as you contemplate this iconic masterpiece.

4. **Discover Sforza Castle (Castello Sforzesco):**
Wander through the courtyards and gardens of this imposing fortress. Visit its various museums, including the Museum of Ancient Art, and admire the striking sculptures and historical artifacts on display.

5. **Immerse Yourself in Art at Brera Art Gallery (Pinacoteca di Brera):**

Explore one of Italy's most prestigious art collections, featuring works by renowned Italian masters. Wander through its galleries, marvel at the exquisite paintings, and appreciate the beauty of this cultural gem.

6. **Experience the Splendor of La Scala Opera House (Teatro alla Scala):**

Attend a performance or take a guided tour of this legendary opera house. Bask in the grandeur of the theater, learn about its illustrious history, and witness world-class opera and ballet performances.

7. **Stroll Through the Navigli District**:

Wander along the picturesque canals of Naviglio Grande and Naviglio Pavese. Browse through vintage shops, visit art galleries, and relax at charming waterfront bars and cafes.

8. **Visit the Leonardo da Vinci National Museum of Science and Technology:**

Explore the interactive exhibits dedicated to science, technology, and the inventions of Leonardo da Vinci. Engage in hands-on activities, marvel at his ingenious creations, and delve into the world of innovation.

9. **Indulge in Shopping at the Quadrilatero della Moda**:

Embark on a shopping spree in Milan's renowned fashion district. Discover luxury boutiques, designer stores, and flagship stores of famous fashion houses on Via Montenapoleone, Via della Spiga, and Via Sant'Andrea.

10. Discover Contemporary Art at the HangarBicocca:
Visit this contemporary art space, housed in a former industrial building, known for its large-scale installations and thought-provoking exhibitions. Experience the cutting-edge works of international contemporary artists.

11. Explore the Natural Beauty of Parco Sempione:
Relax in this sprawling park located behind Sforza Castle. Enjoy a leisurely stroll, have a picnic on the lush lawns, and take in the scenic views of the park's iconic landmarks.

12. Delve into History at the Archaeological Museum of Milan:
Uncover the city's ancient past at this museum, showcasing archaeological artifacts from Roman times to the Middle

Ages. Admire the well-preserved relics and learn about Milan's rich historical heritage.

13. **Taste Local Delicacies at the Food Markets:**

Visit vibrant food markets like *Mercato di Porta Romana* and *Mercato di Via Fauchè*. Sample a variety of Italian cheeses, cured meats, fresh produce, and regional specialties, and savor the flavors of Milanese cuisine.

14. **Enjoy a Performance at the Teatro alla Scala Museum**:

Explore the rich history of the world-famous Teatro alla Scala by visiting its museum. Discover the fascinating backstage secrets, admire the collection of costumes and musical instruments, and learn about the legendary performers who have graced its stage.

15. Discover the Fashion District at the Fashion Library:

Immerse yourself in the world of fashion at the Fashion Library, located in the heart of Milan's fashion district. Browse through an extensive collection of fashion books, magazines, and archives, gaining insight into the evolution of Italian fashion and the industry's impact on Milan's culture.

16. Explore the Historical Ambiance of the Brera District:

Wander through the charming streets of the Brera district, known for its bohemian atmosphere and artistic heritage. Explore the narrow alleys lined with boutique shops, art galleries, and antique dealers. Visit the picturesque Piazza del Carmine, home to the Church of Santa Maria del Carmine with its stunning frescoes.

17. Take a Day Trip to Lake Como:
Escape the city and venture to the breathtaking Lake Como, located just a short distance from Milan. Cruise along the tranquil waters, surrounded by picturesque villas and lush mountains. Explore the charming lakeside towns of Bellagio, Varenna, and Como, each offering their own unique charm and stunning vistas.

18. Experience Milan's Nightlife in the Navigli District:
As the sun sets, head to the vibrant Navigli district to experience Milan's lively nightlife. Explore the bustling bars, trendy nightclubs, and cozy wine bars along the canals. Join the locals in enjoying aperitivo, where you can savor a drink accompanied by a selection of delicious Italian appetizers.

19. Discover the Modern Architecture of Porta Nuova:
Marvel at the contemporary architectural wonders of the Porta Nuova district. Admire the skyscrapers, such as the iconic Bosco Verticale (Vertical Forest), which feature vertical gardens and sustainable design. Take a walk along Corso Como and Corso Garibaldi to discover trendy shops, restaurants, and vibrant street art.

20. Indulge in a Chocolate Experience at the Museo del Cioccolato:
Delight your taste buds at the Museo del Cioccolato (Chocolate Museum). Learn about the history of chocolate, witness the chocolate-making process, and indulge in a variety of delectable treats. Participate in chocolate tastings and

workshops to further enhance your appreciation for this irresistible delight.

Chapter 2

Discovering Venice

Venice, the enchanting city of canals, is a captivating destination nestled in the northeastern region of Italy. Renowned for its unique architectural beauty, rich history, and romantic ambiance, Venice is a true gem of Northern Italy.

The city is built on a group of 118 small islands, connected by a network of canals and charming bridges. Its picturesque waterways, gondolas gliding through narrow canals, and stunning Venetian Gothic palaces create a magical atmosphere that has captivated travelers for centuries.

Venice is famous for its iconic landmarks, the most prominent of which is **Piazza San Marco** (St. Mark's Square). This bustling square is the heart of the city, surrounded by magnificent architectural marvels like St. Mark's Basilica, the Doge's Palace, and the Clock Tower. Admire the intricate Byzantine mosaics, climb the bell tower for panoramic views, and soak in the lively atmosphere of this vibrant gathering place.

Exploring Venice's intricate canal system is an absolute must. Embark on a romantic gondola ride, gliding through narrow canals as you pass beneath picturesque bridges. Let the gondolier serenade you with traditional songs, and immerse yourself in the timeless beauty of this unique cityscape.

Venice is also home to numerous world-class museums and art galleries. _The Gallerie dell'Accademia_ houses a stunning collection of Venetian Renaissance art, showcasing works by masters like Bellini, Titian, and Tintoretto. The Peggy Guggenheim Collection displays an impressive array of modern art in the palatial setting of Palazzo Venier dei Leoni. From classical to contemporary, Venice offers an artistic journey through the ages.

To truly experience the local way of life, wander through the charming neighborhoods of Venice. Lose yourself in the labyrinthine streets of Cannaregio, discover hidden gems in the artistic Dorsoduro, and stroll along the lively promenade of the Zattere. Explore local markets, artisanal shops, and traditional bacari (wine bars) to savor the flavors of

Venetian cuisine. Indulge in local delicacies like fresh seafood, cicchetti (small tapas-style dishes), and the famous Bellini cocktail.

No visit to Venice would be complete without venturing beyond the main islands. Take a vaporetto (water bus) to the nearby islands of Murano, known for its exquisite glassware, and Burano, famous for its vibrant colored houses and intricate lacework. These islands offer a glimpse into traditional craftsmanship and provide a peaceful retreat from the bustling city center.

Venice also hosts a range of vibrant events throughout the year. _The Venetian Carnival,_ with its elaborate masks and costumes, is a spectacle of grandeur and festivity. _The Venice Biennale,_ an internationally renowned art exhibition, attracts artists and art enthusiasts from around the world. These events add an extra layer of cultural richness to the city's already vibrant tapestry.

In Venice, time seems to stand still as you wander through its timeless streets and soak up its unique atmosphere. From the intricate architecture to the gentle lapping of water against the buildings, every moment in Venice feels like a dream. It is a place where romance, art, history, and natural beauty intertwine, leaving an indelible mark on all who visit. Venice truly epitomizes the allure of Northern Italy and beckons travelers to indulge in its unforgettable charm.

Where to Stay

When it comes to choosing where to stay in Venice, you'll find a range of options that cater to different preferences and budgets. From luxurious waterfront hotels to charming bed and breakfasts tucked away in narrow alleys, Venice offers a unique selection of accommodations that allow you to fully immerse yourself in the city's enchanting atmosphere. Here are some suggestions to help you find the perfect place to stay in Venice.

1. San Marco

San Marco is the pulsating heart of Venice, home to iconic landmarks like <u>St. Mark's Square</u> and the Doge's Palace. This central neighborhood is an excellent choice if you want to be close to the main attractions and enjoy the vibrant atmosphere day and night. You'll find a variety of luxury hotels and high-end boutiques in this area, offering stunning views of the canal or the historic buildings.

Recommended hotels in San Marco include the luxurious **Hotel Danieli**, the historic **Baglioni Hotel Luna**, and the boutique **Hotel Concordia**.

2. Cannaregio

Cannaregio is a neighborhood that offers a more authentic Venetian experience. Away from the crowds of the main tourist areas, Cannaregio is known for its local charm, narrow streets, and picturesque canals. Here, you'll find a mix of accommodation options, from budget-friendly guesthouses to boutique hotels with a cozy and intimate ambiance. Explore the neighborhood's hidden gems and savor the local cuisine in traditional trattorias.

Recommended hotels in Cannaregio include the delightful **Hotel Ai Mori d'Oriente,** the family-run Hotel **Antiche Figure**, and the boutique **Hotel Ca' d'Oro**.

3. Dorsoduro

Dorsoduro is a vibrant and bohemian neighborhood known for its art galleries, trendy bars, and lively squares. This area is home to the renowned Accademia Gallery and the Peggy Guggenheim Collection, making it a perfect choice for art enthusiasts. You'll find a mix of stylish boutique hotels and guesthouses, often with unique decor and artistic touches. Enjoy the neighborhood's laid-back vibe and explore its charming streets lined with local shops and cafes.

Recommended hotels in Dorsoduro include the stylish **Hotel Palazzo Stern,** the waterfront **Hotel Canal Grande,** and the unique **Ca' Maria Adele.**

4. San Polo

San Polo is one of the oldest and smallest neighborhoods in Venice, known for its historic charm and local markets. This area offers a more relaxed atmosphere compared to the bustling San Marco. Stay in one of the traditional Venetian palazzos that have been converted into hotels or opt for a family-run bed and breakfast. Enjoy leisurely walks along the Grand Canal, visit the Rialto Market, and indulge in authentic Venetian cuisine in the neighborhood's trattorias.

Recommended hotels in San Polo include the boutique **Hotel Palazzo Barbarigo,** the charming **Al Ponte Antico Hotel**, and the historic Hotel **Rialto.**

5. Castello

Castello is a tranquil neighborhood located towards the eastern part of Venice. If you prefer a quieter and more residential atmosphere, this area is an excellent choice. Castello is home to beautiful parks, charming squares, and local shops. Choose from a range of accommodations, including family-owned inns and charming guesthouses. Experience the local way of life, visit the famous Arsenale, and enjoy panoramic views from the waterfront promenade.

Recommended hotels in Castello include the luxurious **Hotel Metropole,** the waterfront **Hotel Paganelli,** and the historic **Hotel Gabrielli.**

6. Giudecca

Giudecca is an island located just across the canal from the main islands of Venice. Known for its tranquility and panoramic views of the city, Giudecca offers a peaceful retreat away from the crowds. Stay in one of the converted warehouses or modern hotels that offer stunning views of the lagoon. Enjoy the island's waterfront promenade, visit the historic churches, and take a short vaporetto ride to explore the main attractions.

Recommended hotels in Giudecca include the **Hilton Molino Stucky Venice,** the luxurious **Hotel Cipriani,** and the iconic **Belmond Hotel Cipriani.**

7. Lido di Venezia

If you're looking for a beachside escape, consider staying at the Lido di Venezia. This narrow island is known for its sandy beaches, charming promenades, and Art Nouveau villas. Lido offers a range of hotels, including luxurious resorts and boutique accommodations. Enjoy leisurely walks along the beach, rent bicycles and explore the island's picturesque streets. Lido is also home to the famous Venice Film Festival, held annually at the historic Palazzo del Cinema. During the festival, the island comes alive with glitz and glamour, attracting international stars and film enthusiasts from around the world.

Recommended hotels in Lido di Venezia include the **Hotel Excelsior** Venice, the **Grande Albergo Ausonia & Hungaria,** and the charming **Hotel Villa Mabapa.**

Regardless of where you choose to stay in Venice, keep in mind that the city is best explored on foot or by water transport.

Take advantage of the vaporettos (water buses) and water taxis to navigate the canals and reach different parts of the city. Embrace the unique charm of Venice, savor its culinary delights, and let the city's timeless beauty enchant you. Whether you prefer luxury accommodations or cozy guesthouses, Venice offers a range of options to make your stay truly memorable.

What to Eat and Where

Venice, known for its rich culinary tradition, offers a delectable array of dishes that showcase the flavors of the region. From fresh seafood to mouthwatering pasta, here are some must-try dishes and recommended places to indulge in the culinary delights of Venice.

1. Cicchetti

Start your culinary journey with cicchetti, Venice's answer to tapas. These small bites are served in bars and osterias throughout the city. You can enjoy a variety of cicchetti, such as crostini topped with marinated seafood, fried polenta with creamy baccalà (salted cod) spread, or savory meatballs. Head to places like **Cantina Do Mori, Osteria al Squero, or All'Arco** for an authentic cicchetti experience.

2. Risi e Bisi

Risi e bisi is a traditional Venetian dish that consists of creamy risotto cooked with fresh peas. This comforting dish is typically made with local Vialone Nano rice, flavorful broth, and tender peas. Enjoy this classic dish at **Trattoria Da Remigio or Osteria Ai Assassini,** where you can savor the traditional flavors of Venetian cuisine.

3. **Sarde in Saor**

Sarde in saor is a popular Venetian appetizer made with marinated sardines, sweet onions, pine nuts, and raisins. The dish is prepared by frying the sardines and then marinating them in a mixture of vinegar, onions, and spices. The result is a delightful blend of sweet and tangy flavors. Try this Venetian specialty at **Trattoria Antiche Carampane or Osteria Bancogiro.**

4. **Fritto Misto**

Venice's proximity to the sea means that seafood plays a prominent role in its cuisine. Fritto misto is a delectable dish featuring an assortment of lightly battered and fried seafood, including shrimp, calamari, small fish, and soft-shell crab. Sample this seafood delight at **Trattoria da Romano or Osteria da Alberto**.

5. Bigoli in Salsa

Bigoli in salsa is a traditional Venetian pasta dish that features thick, long noodles tossed in a sauce made from slowly stewed onions and salted anchovies. The result is a rich and flavorful combination that perfectly highlights the simplicity of Venetian cuisine. Enjoy this dish at **Trattoria La Madonna or Osteria al Diavolo e l'Acquasanta.**

6. Baccalà Mantecato

Baccalà mantecato is a creamy spread made from salted cod that has been soaked, cooked, and whipped with olive oil, garlic, and parsley. The result is a smooth and flavorful spread that is typically served on crostini or as a filling for sandwiches. Try this traditional dish at **Trattoria Da Fiore or Osteria Alla Frasca.**

7. Tiramisu

Finish off your culinary journey in Venice with a classic Italian dessert, tiramisu. This indulgent treat features layers of espresso-soaked ladyfingers, creamy mascarpone cheese, and a dusting of cocoa powder. Enjoy a heavenly tiramisu at **Pasticceria Tonolo or Osteria Ae Sconte**.

These are just a few highlights of the culinary delights that await you in Venice. As you explore the city, be sure to wander off the beaten path and discover hidden trattorias and local establishments that offer authentic and unforgettable dining experiences.

Tourist Attractions in Venice

Venice, often referred to as the "_Floating City_," is a mesmerizing destination that captivates visitors with its unique charm and captivating beauty. From picturesque canals to stunning architecture, Venice is a treasure trove of tourist attractions that offer a glimpse into its rich history and cultural heritage. Here are some must-visit attractions that will make your trip to Venice truly unforgettable.

1. St. Mark's Square (Piazza San Marco):
St. Mark's Square is the heart of Venice and one of the most iconic squares in the world. It is surrounded by impressive landmarks, including St. Mark's Basilica, the Doge's Palace, and the Campanile (bell tower). Take a leisurely stroll around the square, enjoy a cup of coffee at one of the

historic cafés, and soak in the magnificent atmosphere.

2. **St. Mark's Basilica (Basilica di San Marco):**

A masterpiece of Byzantine architecture, St. Mark's Basilica is an awe-inspiring sight. Adorned with intricate mosaics, marble columns, and golden decorations, the basilica is a symbol of Venice's wealth and power during the Byzantine era. Step inside to admire the stunning interior and don't miss the chance to climb to the terrace for panoramic views of the city.

3. **Doge's Palace (Palazzo Ducale):**

Located adjacent to St. Mark's Basilica, the Doge's Palace is a magnificent palace that served as the residence of the Doge, the ruler of Venice. Explore its opulent rooms, adorned with artwork by renowned painters such as Titian and

Tintoretto. Walk across the Bridge of Sighs, which connects the palace to the prisons, and immerse yourself in the history and grandeur of the Venetian Republic.

4. **Rialto Bridge (Ponte di Rialto):**

Spanning the Grand Canal, the Rialto Bridge is one of Venice's most iconic landmarks. Dating back to the 16th century, this stone bridge offers breathtaking views of the canal and the bustling Rialto Market. Explore the shops and stalls on the bridge, and don't forget to capture the beauty of the bridge from different angles.

5. **Grand Canal (Canal Grande):**

The Grand Canal is the main waterway that winds its way through the heart of Venice. Take a vaporetto (water bus) ride along the canal to witness the stunning palaces, historic buildings, and colorful facades that line its banks. The journey will offer a unique perspective of the city and its enchanting architecture.

6. **Peggy Guggenheim Collection**:
Art enthusiasts should not miss the opportunity to visit the Peggy Guggenheim Collection, housed in the Palazzo Venier dei Leoni. This modern art museum showcases an impressive collection of works by renowned artists such as Picasso, Pollock, and Dalí. Explore the museum's beautiful garden and terrace, which overlooks the Grand Canal.

7. **Bridge of Sighs (Ponte dei Sospiri)**:
The Bridge of Sighs is an iconic and romantic bridge that connects the Doge's Palace to the New Prison. Legend has it that if lovers kiss under the bridge at sunset while riding a gondola, their love

will be eternal. Take a gondola ride or enjoy a stroll along the waterfront to catch a glimpse of this picturesque bridge.

8. **Venetian Gondola Ride:**
A visit to Venice would not be complete without a romantic gondola ride along the city's canals. Drift through narrow waterways, under charming bridges, and soak in the serenity of the city. Gondoliers often sing traditional songs, adding to the enchanting experience.

9. **Murano Island**:
Just a short boat ride from Venice, Murano Island is famous for its centuries-old tradition of glassmaking. Visit the glass factories and witness skilled artisans create intricate glass artworks using traditional techniques. Explore the Murano Glass Museum to learn more about the history and

evolution of glassmaking in Murano. Don't forget to pick up a unique glass souvenir to commemorate your visit.

10. Burano Island:
Another gem in the Venetian lagoon, Burano Island is known for its vibrant and colorful houses. Take a leisurely stroll along the canals and admire the picturesque scenery. Burano is also famous for its lace-making tradition, so be sure to explore the local lace shops and discover the intricate craftsmanship behind this delicate art form.

11. Lido di Venezia:
For a change of pace, head to Lido di Venezia, a barrier island that offers a beautiful sandy beach and a laid-back atmosphere. Enjoy a relaxing day under the sun, go for a swim in the Adriatic Sea, or take a leisurely bike ride along the

island's promenade. Lido is also home to the prestigious Venice Film Festival, held annually in late August or early September.

12. **Scuola Grande di San Rocco:**
Art lovers should visit the Scuola Grande di San Rocco, an impressive building adorned with magnificent artworks by Tintoretto. The walls and ceilings are covered with intricate paintings depicting scenes from the Bible and the life of Saint Roch. Marvel at the masterpieces and admire the artistic genius of Tintoretto.

13. **Jewish Ghetto**:
Explore the historic Jewish Ghetto, which dates back to the 16th century and is one of the oldest Jewish ghettos in Europe. Visit the Jewish Museum to learn about the rich Jewish heritage and history of the area. Don't miss the opportunity to

sample traditional Jewish-Italian cuisine, such as fried artichokes and ricotta-filled pastries, at the local eateries.

14. San Giorgio Maggiore:
Take a short boat ride to the island of San Giorgio Maggiore, located opposite St. Mark's Square. Climb the bell tower of the San Giorgio Maggiore Church for breathtaking panoramic views of Venice. Explore the church's interior, designed by renowned architect Andrea Palladio, and enjoy the peaceful atmosphere of the island.

As you explore these captivating attractions, be sure to wander the narrow streets, get lost in the maze of canals, and embrace the enchanting ambiance of Venice. Immerse yourself in the rich history, art, and culture of this unique city, and let its timeless beauty leave an indelible mark on your heart.

Things to do in Venice

Venice, with its captivating canals, historic landmarks, and romantic atmosphere, offers a plethora of things to do that will make your visit truly memorable. Here are some exciting activities and experiences to enjoy in Venice:

1. Take a Gondola Ride: Glide through the enchanting canals of Venice on a traditional gondola. Let the gondolier serenade you with melodic tunes as you pass by picturesque bridges and charming buildings. It's a quintessential Venetian experience that exudes romance and captures the essence of the city.

2. **Explore St. Mark's Square (Piazza San Marco):**

Wander around the iconic St. Mark's Square, soak in the lively atmosphere, and marvel at the architectural wonders that surround it. Visit St. Mark's Basilica, climb the Campanile for panoramic views, and explore the Doge's Palace to delve into Venice's rich history.

3. **Visit the Rialto Market**:

Immerse yourself in the vibrant atmosphere of the Rialto Market, one of Venice's oldest and most famous markets. Browse through the stalls filled with fresh produce, local seafood, and colorful souvenirs. It's the perfect place to experience the lively energy and flavors of Venetian daily life.

4. Discover the Art of Murano Glassmaking:
Take a boat trip to the island of Murano, renowned for its centuries-old glassmaking tradition. Visit glass factories and watch skilled artisans create intricate glass masterpieces. Don't miss the chance to purchase unique Murano glass souvenirs to take home.

5. Explore the Peggy Guggenheim Collection:
Art lovers should visit the Peggy Guggenheim Collection, an art museum housed in an elegant palace. Admire the impressive collection of modern art, including works by Picasso, Pollock, and Dalí. The museum's beautiful garden and terrace offer a tranquil setting to appreciate the artwork.

6. Get Lost in the Narrow Streets (Calle) and Bridges:

Venice is a city made for wandering. Lose yourself in the labyrinth of narrow streets, known as calles, and cross the charming bridges that connect the various islands. Discover hidden squares, local shops, and quaint cafés along the way.

7. Indulge in Venetian Cuisine:

Venice boasts a rich culinary heritage. Savor traditional dishes like seafood risotto, fegato alla veneziana (liver with onions), and sarde in saor (marinated sardines). Pair your meal with a glass of local wine or a refreshing spritz cocktail. Explore local trattorias and osterias to taste the authentic flavors of Venetian cuisine.

8. Visit the Islands of Burano and Murano:

Take a boat trip to the colorful island of Burano, known for its vibrant houses and intricate lacework. Explore the picturesque streets, visit lace shops, and enjoy delicious seafood in the island's charming restaurants. Additionally, a visit to the island of Murano, famous for its glassmaking heritage, offers a chance to witness artisans at work and explore the island's unique shops.

9. Attend a Classical Music Concert: Venice has a rich musical history, and attending a classical music concert in one of its historic venues is a delightful experience. From intimate chamber performances to grand orchestral concerts, immerse yourself in the enchanting melodies that resonate throughout the city.

10. Take a Vaporetto Ride along the Grand Canal:

Hop on a vaporetto, a public water bus, and cruise along the Grand Canal. Admire the stunning palaces, historic buildings, and picturesque bridges that line the canal. It's a fantastic way to appreciate the grandeur and architectural beauty of Venice.

11. Visit the Jewish Ghetto:

Explore the historic Jewish Ghetto, a significant part of Venice's cultural heritage. Learn about the rich history of the Jewish community and visit the Jewish Museum to delve deeper into their traditions and experiences. Don't miss the opportunity to sample traditional Jewish-Italian cuisine, such as mouthwatering fried artichokes and delectable ricotta-filled pastries, at the local eateries.

12. <u>Enjoy a Sunset Cruise:</u>

Witness the breathtaking beauty of Venice as the sun sets over the shimmering waters. Embark on a sunset cruise along the canals or opt for a romantic gondola ride during the golden hour. Watch as the city's buildings and landmarks glow with a warm, ethereal light, creating a truly magical ambiance.

13. <u>Discover Hidden Gems in the Dorsoduro District</u>:

Explore the charming Dorsoduro district, known for its art galleries, bohemian atmosphere, and beautiful canal views. Visit the Gallerie dell'Accademia, home to an extensive collection of Venetian art from the 14th to 18th centuries. Take a leisurely stroll along the Zattere promenade, offering stunning vistas of the Giudecca Canal.

14. Attend the Venice Carnival:

If you visit during the Carnival season, immerse yourself in the festive spirit of one of the world's most famous carnivals. Witness the colorful costumes, elaborate masks, and lively parades that fill the streets of Venice. Join in the revelry and experience the magic and extravagance of this centuries-old tradition.

15. Relax at Giardini della Biennale:

Find tranquility amidst the hustle and bustle of Venice at the Giardini della Biennale. These beautiful gardens provide a serene escape where you can unwind and enjoy the natural beauty. Admire the sculptures, relax on a bench, or have a picnic surrounded by lush greenery.

16. Take a Day Trip to the Venetian Lagoon Islands:

Venture beyond the main islands of Venice and explore the charming islands of the Venetian Lagoon. Visit the peaceful island of Torcello, known for its ancient churches and tranquil atmosphere. Explore the picturesque island of Sant'Erasmo, famous for its vineyards and agricultural traditions. Each island offers a unique glimpse into the Venetian archipelago's diverse character.

17. **Attend a Mask-Making Workshop**: Unleash your creativity and participate in a traditional Venetian mask-making workshop. Learn about the art of mask-making, its history, and significance in Venetian culture. Design and decorate your own mask, taking home a unique and personalized souvenir of your time in Venice.

Chapter 3

Exploring Verona and the Veneto Region

Verona, situated in the Veneto region of Northern Italy, is a city of rich history, romance, and architectural beauty. As you wander through its ancient streets, you'll discover a tapestry of Roman ruins, medieval structures, and Renaissance palaces that transport you back in time. Verona, known as the setting for Shakespeare's famous play "**Romeo and Juliet**," exudes a captivating charm that attracts visitors from around the world.

The city of Verona is characterized by its well-preserved Roman amphitheater, the

Arena di Verona, which serves as a stunning venue for operatic performances during the annual Verona Opera Festival. This magnificent amphitheater is one of the largest of its kind and offers a unique opportunity to witness world-class opera in an awe-inspiring setting.

Verona's historic center, a UNESCO World Heritage Site, is a treasure trove of architectural wonders. The _Piazza delle Erbe_, a lively square lined with elegant palaces, cafes, and market stalls, is the heart of the city. Here, you can immerse yourself in the vibrant atmosphere, sample local delicacies, and marvel at the stunning frescoes of the Casa Mazzanti.

A visit to Verona wouldn't be complete without a glimpse of Juliet's House (Casa di Giulietta). This iconic landmark is believed to be the inspiration for

Shakespeare's tragic love story. Visitors flock to see the famous balcony where Juliet is said to have declared her love for Romeo. The courtyard is adorned with love notes left by hopeful romantics from all over the world.

Beyond Verona, the Veneto region offers a diverse array of attractions and experiences. From the picturesque shores of _Lake Garda_ to the charming towns of _Padua_ and Vicenza, the Veneto region is a treasure trove of cultural, natural, and gastronomic delights.

The city of **_Padua_** is renowned for its prestigious university, one of the oldest in the world, and its stunning Basilica of Saint Anthony. Explore the historic center, visit the Scrovegni Chapel with its magnificent frescoes by Giotto, and take a stroll through the beautiful Prato della

Valle, one of Europe's largest public squares.

Vicenza, another gem of the Veneto region, is famous for its architectural masterpieces designed by Andrea Palladio. The Palladian Villas, including the Villa Rotonda and the Villa Valmarana ai Nani, showcase Palladio's innovative architectural style and are recognized as UNESCO World Heritage Sites.

Nature lovers will be captivated by the beauty of **Lake Garda**, the largest lake in Italy. Surrounded by picturesque towns and stunning landscapes, Lake Garda offers opportunities for boating, hiking, and exploring charming lakeside villages like Sirmione, Garda, and Malcesine.

The Veneto region is also renowned for its culinary delights. Indulge in the local cuisine, which features dishes like risotto all'Amarone, bigoli pasta with duck ragu, and the famous tiramisu. Pair your meal with a glass of Valpolicella or Prosecco, two of the region's celebrated wines.

Verona and the Veneto region embody the essence of Northern Italy's cultural heritage, architectural splendor, and natural beauty. Whether you're exploring the ancient streets of Verona, admiring Palladio's architectural masterpieces, or savoring the flavors of the region, you're sure to be enchanted by the unique charm and allure of this remarkable part of Italy.

Where to Stay

Verona, with its rich history, romantic ambiance, and architectural wonders, offers a wide range of accommodations to suit every traveler's taste and budget.

From luxurious hotels with stunning views to charming boutique guesthouses tucked away in the city's historic streets, Verona provides a delightful array of options for a memorable stay. Here are some recommended areas and accommodations to consider when choosing where to stay in Verona:

1. Historic Center
Staying in Verona's historic center allows you to immerse yourself in the city's enchanting atmosphere and have easy access to its major attractions. You can choose from a variety of hotels, guesthouses, and apartments that range from budget-friendly to upscale luxury. Some highly recommended options include:

Hotel Accademia: This elegant four-star hotel is located just a few steps from the famous Juliet's House. It offers comfortable rooms, a rooftop terrace with panoramic views, and a central location perfect for exploring the city.

Hotel Antica Porta Leona: Situated near Piazza delle Erbe, this charming hotel occupies a historic building with beautiful frescoes. It features spacious rooms, a courtyard garden, and a cozy lounge area where you can relax after a day of sightseeing.

Residenza Borsari: Located in a 16th-century building, this boutique guesthouse offers stylish rooms with modern amenities. The property is ideally situated near the Arena di Verona and provides a warm and welcoming atmosphere.

2. **San Zeno**:

The San Zeno neighborhood, located just outside the city center, offers a quieter and more residential setting. It's known for its beautiful Basilica of San Zeno Maggiore and its peaceful atmosphere. If you prefer a more tranquil stay away from the bustling city center, consider these accommodation options:

Hotel San Marco Fitness Pool & Spa: This four-star hotel provides comfortable rooms, an outdoor swimming pool, and a wellness center. It's conveniently located near the Basilica of San Zeno Maggiore and offers easy access to the city center by public transportation.

Hotel Villa Malaspina: Set in an elegant 16th-century villa surrounded by a lush garden, this hotel offers a peaceful retreat. It features spacious rooms, an outdoor terrace, and a restaurant serving traditional Italian cuisine.

3. **Borgo Trento:**

Located to the north of the historic center, the Borgo Trento district offers a residential and upscale ambiance. It's known for its tree-lined streets, beautiful villas, and proximity to the Adige River. If you prefer a more residential and luxurious stay, consider these options:

Byblos Art Hotel Villa Amista: This five-star hotel is housed in a renovated 15th-century villa and features an eclectic mix of contemporary art and historic architecture. It offers luxurious rooms, a spa, a gourmet restaurant, and a beautiful garden.

Hotel Giberti: Situated near the Borgo Trento Hospital, this modern hotel provides comfortable rooms, a fitness center, and a rooftop terrace with panoramic views of the city. It's a short walk from the city center and offers convenient access to public transportation.

4. Veronetta:
Located on the opposite side of the Adige River from the historic center, Veronetta is a vibrant neighborhood known for its lively student population. It offers a mix of affordable accommodations, local eateries, and a lively atmosphere. Consider these options for a budget-friendly stay:

B&B La Magnolia: This cozy bed and breakfast offer comfortable rooms, a communal kitchen, and a friendly atmosphere. It's conveniently located near the University of Verona and within walking distance of the city center.

Hotel Martini: Situated near the Ponte Pietra, this budget-friendly hotel offers comfortable rooms at affordable rates. It provides a convenient base for exploring Verona, with the city center just a short walk away. The hotel's friendly staff and cozy atmosphere ensure a pleasant stay.

5. Porta Nuova:

The Porta Nuova neighborhood is situated near Verona's main train station and offers a convenient location for travelers arriving by train. It provides a mix of accommodations, ranging from budget-friendly hotels to upscale options. Consider these choices for a convenient stay near the train station:

Hotel Milano: Located just a few steps from the Porta Nuova train station, this hotel offers comfortable rooms and a welcoming atmosphere. It provides easy access to the city center and serves as a convenient base for exploring Verona and its surroundings.

Hotel Leopardi: Situated a short distance from the train station, this modern hotel features comfortable rooms, a restaurant, and a rooftop terrace with panoramic views of the city. It offers a peaceful retreat while still being within reach of Verona's major attractions.

6. Borgo Roma:
The Borgo Roma neighborhood is located southwest of the city center and offers a more residential setting. It's a good option for those seeking affordable accommodations away from the tourist

crowds. Consider these options for a comfortable and budget-friendly stay:

Hotel Maxim: Situated near Verona's Exhibition Center, this hotel offers comfortable rooms, a restaurant, and free parking. It provides easy access to the city center by public transportation and is a convenient choice for business travelers.

Hotel Gardenia: Located in a quiet residential area, this family-run hotel offers cozy rooms and a friendly atmosphere. It's well-connected to the city center by public transportation and provides a peaceful retreat after a day of exploring Verona.

It doesn't matter where you choose to stay in Verona, surely you'll be captivated by the city's charm, rich history, and architectural beauty. Whether it's a luxurious hotel in the heart of the historic center or a cozy bed and breakfast in a quieter neighborhood, Verona offers a range of accommodations to suit every traveler's preferences.

What to Eat and Where

Verona, located in the Veneto region of Northern Italy, is renowned for its culinary delights. From traditional Italian dishes to regional specialties, Verona offers a gastronomic journey that will satisfy even the most discerning palates. Here are some must-try dishes and recommended places to eat in Verona:

1. Tortellini di Valeggio:
These delicate pasta pockets filled with a combination of meat, cheese, and herbs are a local specialty. Head to **Ristorante Alla Borsa,** located in the historic center,

to savor authentic Tortellini di Valeggio prepared with care and served in a flavorful broth.

2. **Pastissada de Caval**:

This hearty dish is a true Veronese classic. It features slow-cooked horse meat stewed in red wine, spices, and aromatic herbs. **_Ristorante Maffei_**, situated near Piazza delle Erbe, is known for its excellent Pastissada de Caval, showcasing the rich flavors of this traditional Veronese dish.

3. **Bigoli con l'Anatra**:

Bigoli, a type of thick spaghetti, paired with succulent duck ragu. Ristorante Greppia offers a delectable rendition of Bigoli con l'Anatra, where the homemade pasta is cooked to perfection and served with a flavorful duck sauce.

4. Risotto all'Amarone:

Verona is located in the heart of the Valpolicella wine region, famous for its Amarone wine. Risotto all'Amarone combines the richness of this robust red wine with creamy Arborio rice, creating a luscious and indulgent dish. For an exceptional dining experience, visit **Osteria Sottoriva**, a charming restaurant known for its excellent risotto.

5. Polenta e Osei:

Polenta, a staple of Northern Italian cuisine, takes center stage in this unique dessert. It features a sweet polenta cake topped with marzipan birds, representing the traditional hunting culture of the region. Visit **Pasticceria Flego**, a historic pastry shop, to sample their delightful Polenta e Osei and indulge in other tempting treats.

6. <u>Amarone Wine Tasting</u>:
Verona is the gateway to the Valpolicella wine region, renowned for its Amarone wine. Take the opportunity to visit local wineries and indulge in a wine tasting experience. **<u>Cantina Valpolicella</u>** Negrar and Allegrini are among the notable wineries where you can savor the rich, full-bodied flavors of Amarone wine.

7. <u>Gelato from Gelateria Ponte Pietra</u>:
Treat yourself to a scoop or probably two of artisan gelato from **<u>Gelateria Ponte Pietra,</u>** located near the picturesque Ponte Pietra bridge. Choose from a variety of mouthwatering flavors, made with the finest ingredients. Whether you prefer classic options like chocolate and pistachio or more adventurous combinations, Gelateria Ponte Pietra has something to delight every gelato lover.

8. Caffè Dante Biscotti:

As you wander through Verona, make a stop at Caffè Dante, a historic café known for its delicious homemade biscotti. Pair these delectable cookies with a traditional Italian espresso or cappuccino for a delightful mid-day treat.

9. Trattoria Sottoriva:

For a truly authentic Veronese dining experience, head to Trattoria Sottoriva. This cozy trattoria is known for its traditional dishes prepared with locally sourced ingredients. Indulge in classic Veronese recipes such as Bollito Misto (mixed boiled meats) and Pearà, a creamy sauce made with bread crumbs, beef marrow, and spices.

From traditional dishes to innovative creations, Verona's restaurants and eateries provide a culinary journey that will leave you with a deep appreciation for the flavors of Northern Italy. Explore the city's diverse dining options, indulge in local specialties, and savor the delightful culinary delights that Verona has to offer.

Tourist Attractions in Verona

Verona, a city steeped in history and romance, offers a wealth of captivating tourist attractions that draw visitors from around the world. From ancient Roman ruins to stunning Renaissance architecture, Verona showcases its rich heritage at every turn. Here are some of the top tourist attractions in Verona that will transport you back in time and leave you awe-inspired:

1. Arena di Verona:
One of Verona's most iconic landmarks, Arena di Verona, a magnificent Roman

amphitheater that dates back to the 1st century AD. This well-preserved structure is renowned for its annual opera performances during the Verona Arena Opera Festival. Explore the grand arena, admire its impressive architecture, and imagine the grand spectacles that once took place within its walls.

2. Piazza delle Erbe:

Located in the heart of Verona's historic center, Piazza delle Erbe is a vibrant square surrounded by beautiful historic buildings. It was once the site of the Roman Forum and now serves as a lively gathering place. Explore the bustling market stalls, admire the well-preserved frescoes of the Mazzanti Houses, and relax at one of the many cafes to soak in the atmosphere.

3. Juliet's House (Casa di Giulietta):

Verona's association with Shakespeare's tragic love story, Romeo and Juliet, has made Juliet's House a popular tourist attraction. Visit the 14th-century house believed to have belonged to the Capulet family and stand on the famous balcony where Juliet is said to have declared her love for Romeo. Leave a love letter on the walls and explore the courtyard adorned with statues.

4. Piazza Bra:

Piazza Bra is one of the largest squares in Italy and serves as a vibrant gathering place for locals and visitors alike. Take a leisurely stroll along the square, marvel at the imposing Portoni della Bra city gates, and admire the Palazzo della Gran Guardia. Enjoy a coffee or gelato at one of the charming cafes and soak in the atmosphere of this lively square.

5. Castelvecchio:

Castelvecchio, a medieval castle built in the 14th century, is an architectural masterpiece and now houses a museum. Explore the castle's fortified walls, towers, and the Ponte Scaligero, a fortified bridge that spans the Adige River. Inside the museum, discover an impressive collection of medieval and Renaissance art, including works by Veronese painters.

6. Basilica di San Zeno Maggiore:

This Romanesque masterpiece is dedicated to Verona's patron saint, San Zeno. The Basilica di San Zeno Maggiore showcases stunning architecture, intricate details, and beautiful frescoes. Admire the bronze doors depicting biblical scenes, visit the crypt where the saint's relics are housed, and take in the peaceful atmosphere of the basilica and its surrounding gardens.

7. Giardino Giusti:

Escape the bustling city and immerse yourself in the tranquility of Giardino Giusti, a stunning Renaissance garden. Explore the beautifully landscaped terraces, intricate labyrinth, and enjoy panoramic views of Verona from the elevated vantage points. The garden's serene atmosphere and meticulously manicured landscapes make it a delightful oasis to relax and unwind.

8. Ponte Pietra:

Ponte Pietra is Verona's oldest bridge and a testament to the city's rich history. This Roman bridge offers breathtaking views of the Adige River and the surrounding architecture. Take a leisurely walk across the bridge and admire its elegant arches, which have been meticulously restored over the centuries.

9. Scaliger Tombs (Arche Scaligere):

The Scaliger Tombs are a collection of Gothic funerary monuments built for Verona's ruling Scaligeri family. These ornate tombs, located near the Church of Santa Maria Antica, are adorned with intricate sculptures and elaborate details. Each tomb is dedicated to a different member of the Scaligeri dynasty, and they serve as a remarkable testament to the family's power and influence during the Middle Ages.

10. Teatro Romano:

Situated on the banks of the Adige River, the Teatro Romano is an ancient Roman theater that once hosted grand theatrical performances. Although partially ruined, the theater's remains are still impressive, with its stone seating, stage, and backdrop offering glimpses into its former glory. The adjacent archaeological museum provides further insights into Verona's Roman past.

11. Museo di Castelvecchio:

Housed within the Castelvecchio complex, the Museo di Castelvecchio is an art museum that showcases a vast collection of medieval and Renaissance artwork. Explore the museum's halls to admire sculptures, paintings, ceramics, and other artifacts. Highlights include works by famous Italian artists like Pisanello, Mantegna, and Bellini.

12. Porta Borsari:

Porta Borsari is a well-preserved Roman gate that once served as an entrance to the ancient city of Verona. This monumental structure, adorned with arches and decorative reliefs, stands as a testament to Verona's rich Roman history.

Take a moment to appreciate its grandeur and imagine the hustle and bustle that would have passed through its gates in ancient times.

13. **Museo di Storia Naturale**:

The Museo di Storia Naturale (Natural History Museum) offers a fascinating exploration of the natural world. From dinosaur fossils to geological specimens, the museum's exhibits showcase the diversity of life on Earth. Learn about Verona's geological past, discover the region's flora and fauna, and gain insights into the natural world through interactive displays and educational exhibits.

14. **Sant'Anastasia**:

Sant'Anastasia is a stunning Gothic church that dominates Verona's skyline with its towering bell tower and intricate facade. Step inside to marvel at the spacious interior, adorned with beautiful frescoes, intricate woodwork, and a breathtaking high altar. Climb the bell tower for panoramic views of Verona and the surrounding area.

15. Verona Cathedral (Duomo di Verona):
The Verona Cathedral, also known as the Duomo di Verona, is a Romanesque masterpiece that showcases a blend of architectural styles. Admire its stunning facade, adorned with intricate reliefs and sculptures. Step inside to explore the cathedral's impressive interior, including the ornate chapels and the Chapel of St. Helen, which houses the relics of Verona's patron saint.

Verona's rich history, architectural wonders, and artistic treasures make it a city brimming with captivating tourist attractions. Whether you're exploring ancient Roman ruins, admiring Gothic monuments, or immersing yourself in Renaissance art, Verona offers a fascinating journey through time and culture. Discover the city's enchanting attractions and let Verona's unique charm captivate your heart.

Things to do in Verona

Verona, a city steeped in history and romance, offers a plethora of activities and experiences that cater to every visitor's interests. From exploring ancient ruins to immersing oneself in cultural events, Verona presents a diverse range of things to do. Here are some top recommendations for things to do in Verona:

1. Explore the Historic Center:

Begin your Verona adventure by exploring the city's historic center, a UNESCO World Heritage site. Wander through the picturesque cobblestone streets, marvel at the beautifully preserved medieval architecture, and soak in the charming atmosphere. Admire the grand Piazza delle Erbe, visit the imposing Scaliger Tombs, and discover hidden gems around every corner.

2. Visit Juliet's House (Casa di Giulietta):
Pay a visit to Juliet's House, a famous landmark associated with Shakespeare's tragic love story, Romeo and Juliet. Stand on the iconic balcony, touch the bronze statue of Juliet for good luck, and leave a love note on the walls of the courtyard. The house is also home to a museum that showcases artifacts related to the play and the enduring tale of star-crossed lovers.

3. Attend an Opera Performance at the Arena di Verona:

Immerse yourself in the magic of opera by attending a performance at the Arena di Verona. This ancient Roman amphitheater provides a breathtaking setting for open-air opera shows. From *June to September*, the Verona Arena Opera Festival showcases world-class performances, attracting opera enthusiasts from around the globe. Experience the power and beauty of operatic performances against the backdrop of this remarkable venue.

4. Climb Torre dei Lamberti:

Ascend the Torre dei Lamberti, the tallest tower in Verona, for panoramic views of the city and its surroundings. From the top, you'll be treated to breathtaking vistas that encompass the historic center, the River Adige, and the surrounding hills. The climb may be a bit challenging, but the views from the top are well worth it.

5. Discover the Roman Theater (Teatro Romano) and Archaeological Museum:
Explore Verona's rich Roman heritage at the Teatro Romano and its adjacent archaeological museum. Walk among the ancient ruins of the Roman theater, where performances were held centuries ago. Marvel at the well-preserved structures, including the stage, seating, and backdrop. The nearby museum provides further insights into Verona's Roman past, displaying artifacts and exhibits that showcase the city's ancient history.

6. Take a Stroll Along the Adige River:
Enjoy a leisurely walk along the banks of the Adige River, which runs through the heart of Verona. Admire the picturesque

bridges, capture stunning views of the city's architecture reflected in the water, and revel in the peaceful ambiance. Several charming riverside cafes and restaurants offer the perfect spots to relax, sip a coffee, and watch the world go by.

7. **Visit the Verona Cathedral (Duomo di Verona)**:

Enter the magnificent Verona Cathedral, a Romanesque masterpiece that boasts impressive architecture and exquisite artwork. Explore the stunning interior, adorned with frescoes, sculptures, and beautiful stained glass windows. Don't miss the Chapel of St. Helen, which houses the relics of Verona's patron saint.

8. **Wander through Giardino Giusti**:

Escape the bustling city and step into the tranquility of Giardino Giusti, a

Renaissance garden that offers a peaceful retreat. Discover the meticulously landscaped terraces, charming pathways, and fragrant rose gardens. Climb the garden's panoramic tower for breathtaking views of Verona and its surrounding hills.

9. Visit the Museo di Castelvecchio:
Delve into Verona's art and history at the Museo di Castelvecchio, housed within the medieval Castelvecchio fortress. This impressive museum showcases a vast collection of art, sculptures, and artifacts spanning various periods, including medieval, Renaissance, and modern art. Admire works by renowned artists such as Mantegna and Bellini, and explore the castle's fortified walls, towers, and the Ponte Scaligero, a fortified bridge that spans the Adige River.

10. Experience Verona's Culinary Delights:

Indulge in the culinary delights of Verona, which are sure to tantalize your taste buds. Sample regional specialties such as "risotto all'Amarone" (risotto cooked with Amarone wine), "pastissada de caval" (horse meat stew), and "tortellini di Valeggio" (stuffed pasta). Pair your meal with a glass of Valpolicella or Soave, renowned local wines. Explore the city's charming osterias, trattorias, and enotecas, and savor the authentic flavors of Veronese cuisine.

11. Take a Wine Tour in the Valpolicella Region:

Embark on a wine tour through the picturesque Valpolicella wine region, located just outside Verona. Visit vineyards and wineries, learn about the winemaking process, and indulge in tastings of Valpolicella, Amarone, and Recioto wines. Enjoy the scenic landscapes of rolling hills and vineyards, and gain a deeper appreciation for the region's winemaking traditions.

12. Attend a Cultural Event or Festival:
Verona is known for its vibrant cultural scene and hosts a variety of events and festivals throughout the year. Experience the Verona Jazz Festival, which brings world-class jazz musicians to the city, or the Verona Summer Theater Festival, showcasing open-air performances in historic venues. During the Christmas season, explore the Verona Christmas Market and immerse yourself in the festive atmosphere.

13. Shop for Italian Fashion and Souvenirs:

Verona offers excellent shopping opportunities, whether you're looking for high-end fashion or unique local crafts. Explore the luxury boutiques and designer stores along Via Mazzini and Via Cappello, or browse the local markets for handmade goods, jewelry, and souvenirs. Don't forget to pick up a bottle of olive oil, traditional Veronese ceramics, or a box of "baci di Giulietta" (Juliet's kisses) chocolates.

14. Take a Bike Ride along the River Adige:

Rent a bike and enjoy a scenic ride along the River Adige's picturesque cycling paths. Explore the outskirts of Verona, pedal through vineyards and orchards, and discover charming villages in the surrounding countryside. Cycling is a fantastic way to enjoy the natural beauty of the region while staying active.

15. Attend a Performance at Teatro Filarmonico:

Immerse yourself in the performing arts by attending a concert or opera performance at Teatro Filarmonico. This historic theater hosts a variety of musical performances, including classical music, opera, and ballet. Experience the magic of live performances in an elegant setting, and enjoy the incredible talent showcased on stage.

Verona offers a diverse range of activities that cater to every interest. Whether you're a history enthusiast, an art lover, a foodie, or a nature lover, Verona has something to captivate and inspire you. Embrace the city's rich heritage, immerse yourself in its cultural offerings, and create unforgettable memories in this enchanting destination.

Chapter 4

Turin and the Piedmont Region

Nestled in the northwestern corner of Italy, Turin and the Piedmont region beckon travelers with their unique blend of history, culture, and breathtaking landscapes. From magnificent architecture and world-class cuisine to rolling hills and majestic mountains, this region offers a wealth of experiences for every visitor. Let's delve into the captivating overview of Turin and the Piedmont region:

Turin
As the capital city of the Piedmont region, Turin exudes elegance and charm. Known for its rich history as the former capital of

the Kingdom of Italy, Turin boasts a wealth of architectural treasures and cultural landmarks. Stroll through the city's grand boulevards, adorned with majestic palaces and opulent squares, and soak in the grandeur of this regal city.

The city's most iconic symbol is the <u>Mole Antonelliana</u>, a towering structure that houses the National Cinema Museum. Ascend to its observation deck for panoramic views of Turin's skyline and the stunning backdrop of the surrounding Alps. Explore the historic center with its Baroque-style buildings, picturesque piazzas, and bustling café culture. Don't miss the Turin Cathedral, which houses the famous Shroud of Turin, a Christian relic believed to bear the image of Jesus Christ.

Turin is also renowned for its chocolate and café culture. Indulge in a cup of rich, velvety hot chocolate at one of the city's historic cafes, such as Caffè Al Bicerin. Delight your taste buds with the city's signature sweet treat, gianduiotti, delicious chocolates made with hazelnut paste. And for a true culinary adventure, savor the local specialty, bagna cauda, a warm dipping sauce served with an assortment of fresh vegetables.

Piedmont Region

Beyond Turin, the Piedmont region unfolds with its breathtaking landscapes and gastronomic delights. Piedmont offers a culinary journey that celebrates local produce and traditional recipes.

Explore the picturesque Langhe wine region, dotted with vineyards and charming hilltop villages, and indulge in wine tastings and cellar tours.

Nature lovers will find solace in the Piedmont region's stunning natural beauty. Discover the peaceful shores of Lake Maggiore, where pristine waters meet picturesque towns and enchanting islands. Explore the idyllic countryside of the Monferrato region, characterized by rolling hills adorned with vineyards and dotted with medieval castles and charming villages. And for outdoor enthusiasts, the majestic peaks of the Italian Alps offer opportunities for hiking, skiing, and breathtaking alpine vistas.

History and culture thrive in Piedmont's cities and towns. Visit the UNESCO-listed Royal Residences of Turin, a collection of palaces and gardens that once served as the Savoy dynasty's residences. Marvel at the architectural splendor of the *Reggia di Venaria, the Palazzo Reale*, and the *Palazzo Madama*. Discover the medieval charm of towns like Alba, with its annual truffle festival, and Asti, famous for its sparkling wines and the Palio horse race.

In Piedmont, tradition and innovation blend seamlessly, making it a region that cherishes its heritage while embracing modernity. From the refined elegance of Turin to the tranquil beauty of its countryside, the Piedmont region invites visitors to immerse themselves in its rich history, indulge in its culinary delights, and marvel at its natural wonders. Prepare to be captivated by the timeless allure of Turin and the enchanting Piedmont region.

Where to Stay

When it comes to finding the perfect place to stay in Turin and the Piedmont region, you'll be spoiled for choice. From luxury hotels to cozy bed and breakfasts, there are accommodations to suit every traveler's taste and budget. Here are some recommended neighborhoods and accommodations to consider:

1. Turin City Center:
Stay in the heart of the city, close to major attractions and cultural landmarks. Choose from a range of stylish boutique hotels and renowned luxury establishments. Some notable options include **Grand Hotel Sitea**, **NH Collection Torino Piazza Carlina**, and **Hotel Victoria**.

2. Lingotto:

This district, located in the southern part of Turin, offers a mix of modernity and history. It's known for the iconic Lingotto building, a former Fiat factory transformed into a cultural center. Stay at **NH Torino Lingotto Congres**s, which combines contemporary design with historical elements.

3. San Salvario:
Known for its vibrant nightlife and bohemian atmosphere, San Salvario is a popular neighborhood for young travelers. Explore its lively streets filled with trendy bars, restaurants, and artistic venues. Consider accommodations such as **Tomato Backpackers Hotel** and **Art Hotel Boston.**

4. Asti:
If you're planning to explore the wine country of Piedmont, consider staying in

the charming town of Asti. Surrounded by vineyards and historic buildings, Asti offers a serene setting and easy access to renowned wineries. Suggested accommodations include **Hotel Palio** and **Hotel Rainero.**

5. Alba:

Alba is another delightful town in the Piedmont region, famous for its truffles and wine. Immerse yourself in the picturesque streets, visit the local markets, and indulge in culinary delights. For a memorable stay, check out **Hotel Calissano** and **Hotel Langhe.**

6. Lake Maggiore:

For a tranquil lakeside retreat, head to Lake Maggiore and its surrounding towns such as Stresa and Verbania. Enjoy the serene views, explore the botanical gardens, and relax in luxurious waterfront hotels. Recommended options include **Grand Hotel Des Iles Borromees**, **Hotel Villa e Palazzo Aminta**, and **Hotel Belvedere**.

7. Countryside Retreats:
To immerse yourself in the Piedmont countryside, consider staying at agriturismos, which are traditional farmhouses offering comfortable accommodations and a chance to experience rural life. **Agriturismo Cascina Papaveri** near Alba and **Agriturismo Tenuta La Romana** near Asti are excellent choices.

These are just a few recommendations to get you started, but there are numerous other accommodations available throughout Turin and the Piedmont region. Whether you prefer the hustle and bustle of the city or the tranquility of the countryside, you're sure to find the perfect place to make your stay in Northern Italy truly memorable.

What to Eat and Where

When it comes to dining in Turin and the Piedmont region, prepare yourself for a culinary journey that celebrates the region's rich gastronomic traditions and local flavors. Piedmont is renowned for its exquisite cuisine, which combines hearty ingredients, seasonal produce, and a touch of elegance. Here are some must-try dishes and recommended dining spots to satisfy your taste buds:

1. Bagna Cauda:
Indulge in the iconic Piedmontese dish of bagna cauda, a warm dipping sauce made with anchovies, garlic, olive oil, and butter. Enjoy it with a selection of fresh,

crisp vegetables like cardoons, artichokes, and peppers. Sample this traditional delight at **Ristorante Del Cambio** or **Ristorante Consorzio**.

2. **Tajarin al Tartufo:**
Piedmont is famous for its truffles, and one of the best ways to savor their aroma and flavor is through tajarin al tartufo. These thin, handmade egg noodles are dressed with a rich butter and truffle sauce. For an unforgettable truffle experience, visit **Ristorante La Piola** or **Ristorante Tre Galline.**

3. **Agnolotti del Plin:**
Another pasta specialty of the region, agnolotti del plin are small, stuffed pasta parcels usually filled with meat, spinach, or cheese. Enjoy these delicate morsels served with butter and sage or a meat-based sauce. **Ristorante Del Cambio**

and **Ristorante Consorzio** are excellent places to try this classic dish.

4. Brasato al Barolo:
Piedmontese cuisine is known for its succulent meat dishes, and brasato al Barolo is a prime example. This slow-cooked beef braised in Barolo wine develops a rich, savory flavor. Savor this dish at **Ristorante Del Cambio** or **Ristorante Tre Galline**.

5. Finanziera:
For those seeking a unique culinary experience, try finanziera. This traditional Piedmontese dish features an assortment of offal meats, such as sweetbreads, chicken livers, and veal brains, cooked with aromatic herbs and served in a flavorful sauce. **Ristorante Tre Galline** is a great place to sample this regional specialty.

6. Gelato and Pastries:
Indulge your sweet tooth with Piedmont's delectable desserts. Enjoy gelato at Gelateria La Romana or Gelateria Pepino, known for their artisanal flavors. Savor traditional pastries like baci di dama (hazelnut cookies), torta di nocciole (hazelnut cake), and bonèt (chocolate and amaretto pudding) at **Pasticceria Gertosio** or **Pasticceria Reale**.

7. Winery Visits:
No visit to Piedmont is complete without exploring its renowned wine regions. Take a trip to Barolo, Barbaresco, or Asti and indulge in wine tastings at local wineries. Visit **Cascina Bruciata**, **Marchesi di Gresy**, or **Michele Chiarlo** for a memorable wine experience.

8. Traditional Osterias and Trattorias:

To truly experience Piedmontese cuisine in an authentic setting, dine at traditional osterias and trattorias. These cozy, family-run establishments serve regional specialties with a warm, welcoming atmosphere. Visit **Osteria del Boccondivino** or **Trattoria Valenza** for a taste of local hospitality.

Remember, this is just a small taste of the culinary delights that await you in Turin and the Piedmont region. Don't hesitate to explore local markets, seek recommendations from locals, and try new dishes that pique your curiosity.

Tourist Attractions in Turin and the Piedmont Region

Turin and the Piedmont region are home to a wealth of fascinating tourist attractions that showcase the area's rich history, art, culture, and natural beauty. From grand palaces and museums to picturesque landscapes and charming towns, there's something for everyone to explore and admire. Here are some of the top tourist attractions in Turin and the Piedmont region:

1. **Mole Antonelliana (Turin):**

This iconic landmark of Turin houses the National Cinema Museum and offers panoramic views of the city. Marvel at its distinctive architecture and explore the museum's collection dedicated to the history of cinema.

2. **Egyptian Museum (Turin):**

Known as one of the most important museums of its kind in the world, the Egyptian Museum houses an extensive collection of ancient Egyptian artifacts, including mummies, statues, and tomb reliefs.

3. **Royal Palace of Turin (Turin):**
Step into the lavish world of the Savoy dynasty by visiting the Royal Palace. Explore its opulent rooms, admire the beautiful architecture, and learn about the history of the Italian monarchy.

4. **Reggia di Venaria (Turin):**
This grand palace complex, located just outside Turin, is a UNESCO World Heritage site. Explore the stunning gardens, visit the elegant interiors, and immerse yourself in the royal splendor of the past.

5. **Sacra di San Michele (Turin):**
Perched atop Mount Pirchiriano, the Sacra di San Michele is a breathtaking abbey that dates back to the 10th century.

Visit this spiritual and architectural gem and enjoy panoramic views of the surrounding landscape.

6. Langhe Wine Region (Piedmont):

Embark on a wine tour through the picturesque Langhe region, known for its vineyards, rolling hills, and charming villages. Visit renowned wineries, indulge in wine tastings, and savor the flavors of the famous Barolo and Barbaresco wines.

7. Lake Maggiore (Piedmont):

Discover the beauty of Lake Maggiore, a stunning lake shared between Piedmont and Lombardy. Explore the Borromean Islands with their enchanting gardens and palaces, take a boat ride on the lake, or simply relax in the serene surroundings.

8. Alba (Piedmont):

Known as the capital of the Langhe region, Alba is famous for its truffles and fine wines. Explore the medieval streets, visit the truffle markets, and indulge in the local gastronomy at charming restaurants and cafes.

9. Asti (Piedmont):

Experience the medieval charm of Asti, known for its sparkling wines and historic landmarks. Explore the Gothic-style Asti Cathedral, admire the Torre Troyana, and immerse yourself in the lively atmosphere of the Palio horse race.

10. Sacro Monte di Varallo (Piedmont):

Located in the Sesia Valley, Sacro Monte di Varallo is a pilgrimage site featuring a series of chapels and statues depicting scenes from the life of Christ. Take a scenic walk through the hillside complex and admire the artistic and religious significance.

11. **Venaria Reale (Piedmont):**

Visit the town of Venaria Reale and explore its stunning Royal Palace, vast gardens, and intricate fountains. The palace complex offers guided tours and exhibitions that showcase the grandeur and history of the House of Savoy.

12. **Canavese Region (Piedmont):**

Explore the Canavese region, known for its charming towns, vineyards, and historical sites. Visit the medieval fortress of Ivrea, stroll through the streets of San Giorgio Canavese, and enjoy the natural beauty of the area.

13. **Sacro Monte di Oropa (Piedmont):**

Discover the majestic Sacro Monte di Oropa, a UNESCO World Heritage site located near Biella. This sacred mountain is dotted with a series of chapels dedicated to the Virgin Mary, offering a spiritual and serene experience. Take a peaceful walk along the path, admire the beautiful artwork, and soak in the tranquil atmosphere.

14. Ivrea (Piedmont):

Explore the charming town of Ivrea, known for its rich history and architectural gems. Visit the striking Ivrea Cathedral, stroll through the medieval streets of the Old Town, and learn about the town's industrial heritage at the Olivetti Typewriter Museum.

15. Vercelli (Piedmont):

Discover the city of Vercelli, renowned for its rice production and historical landmarks. Visit the Basilica of Sant'Andrea, an impressive example of

Romanesque architecture, and explore the city's lively squares, elegant palaces, and picturesque streets.

16. Rivoli Castle (Turin):

Located in the town of Rivoli, just outside Turin, the Rivoli Castle is a magnificent example of Baroque architecture. Discover contemporary art exhibitions within the castle's walls and enjoy the panoramic views from its terrace.

17. Superga Basilica (Turin):

Situated atop the Superga Hill, the Superga Basilica offers panoramic views of Turin and the surrounding countryside. Visit this beautiful church, which also serves as a royal mausoleum, and explore its history and architectural splendor.

18. Serralunga d'Alba Castle (Piedmont):

Venture to the village of Serralunga d'Alba, where you'll find the impressive Serralunga d'Alba Castle. This medieval fortress is known for its distinctive cylindrical shape and offers guided tours that take you back in time.

19. **Piedmontese Alps:**

Nature enthusiasts will appreciate the stunning landscapes of the Piedmontese Alps. Embark on hiking or skiing adventures in areas like the Gran Paradiso National Park, Valle d'Aosta, or the Monte Rosa Massif, and revel in the beauty of the alpine scenery.

20. **Turin Shroud (Turin):**

For those interested in religious artifacts, the Turin Shroud is an important pilgrimage site. Located in Turin's Cathedral of Saint John the Baptist, the shroud is believed to bear the image of

Jesus Christ and attracts visitors from around the world.

These are just a few of the many incredible tourist attractions that await you in Turin and the Piedmont region. From cultural landmarks and historical sites to natural wonders and culinary delights, there is something to captivate every traveler's interest. Immerse yourself in the beauty, history, and flavors of this remarkable part of Northern Italy.

Things to do in Turin and the Piedmont Region

When visiting Turin and the Piedmont region, you'll find a diverse range of activities to enjoy, whether you're a history buff, a nature enthusiast, a food lover, or an art aficionado. Here are some of the top things to do in Turin and the Piedmont region:

1. Explore the Historic Center of Turin:
Take a leisurely stroll through the charming streets of Turin's historic center. Admire the beautiful architecture, visit historical landmarks like Piazza Castello and Palazzo Madama, and soak in the vibrant atmosphere of this elegant city.

2. Visit the Turin Cathedral and the Holy Shroud:
Discover the Turin Cathedral, home to the famous Holy Shroud. Explore the cathedral's interior, learn about its history, and contemplate the significance of this religious relic.

3. Delve into Art and History at the Royal Museums:

Turin is home to several impressive museums. Visit the Royal Palace of Turin to explore its extensive art collection, including works by renowned artists. Don't miss the Royal Armoury, which houses a remarkable collection of arms and armor.

4. **Indulge in Chocolate at Turin's Historic Cafés**:

Turin is renowned for its rich chocolate tradition. Treat yourself to a visit to historic cafés such as Caffè Al Bicerin or Caffè Mulassano, and savor delicious hot chocolate or local specialty chocolates.

5. **Explore the Venaria Reale:**

Venture just outside Turin to the Venaria Reale, a magnificent royal palace complex. Explore the stunning gardens, visit the opulent interiors, and learn about the fascinating history of the House of Savoy.

6. Experience the Wonders of the Egyptian Museum:
Immerse yourself in the ancient world at the Egyptian Museum, one of the most important collections of Egyptian artifacts in the world. Marvel at the exhibits, including mummies, statues, and hieroglyphic inscriptions.

7. Discover the Wine Region of Langhe:
Embark on a wine tasting tour in the picturesque Langhe region, known for its vineyards and charming hilltop villages. Sample exquisite wines such as Barolo and Barbaresco, and enjoy the beautiful landscapes.

8. Visit the Sacra di San Michele:
Take a trip to the Sacra di San Michele, a stunning abbey perched on Mount Pirchiriano. Enjoy panoramic views of the

surrounding landscape, explore the abbey's interior, and soak in the spiritual ambiance.

9. Explore the Lakes of Piedmont:
Discover the enchanting lakes of Piedmont, such as Lake Maggiore and Lake Orta. Take a boat ride, visit the charming lakeside towns, and relax in the peaceful surroundings.

10. Indulge in Piedmontese Cuisine:
Don't miss the opportunity to taste the delicious Piedmontese cuisine. Savor traditional dishes like agnolotti pasta, brasato al Barolo (braised beef in Barolo wine), and gianduja chocolate. Dine in local trattorias or Michelin-starred restaurants for a culinary experience to remember.

11. Ski or Hike in the Piedmontese Alps:

If you enjoy outdoor activities, head to the Piedmontese Alps for skiing, snowboarding, or hiking. Explore the scenic trails, breathe in the fresh mountain air, and take in the breathtaking views.

12. **Discover the Charm of Piedmontese Towns**:

Visit picturesque towns such as Alba, Asti, and Saluzzo. Wander through their historic centers, admire the architecture, and immerse yourself in the local culture.

13. **Attend Festivals and Events**:

Check the calendar for festivals and events happening during your visit. Experience the lively atmosphere of events like the Turin International Book Fair, the Alba Truffle Fair, or the Ivrea Carnival. Immerse yourself in the local traditions, enjoy live performances, and participate in the festivities.

14. Take a Bike Ride along the Po River:
Rent a bike and explore the scenic paths along the Po River. Enjoy a leisurely ride, stop at charming riverside towns, and admire the natural beauty of the surrounding landscapes.

15. Visit the Basilica of Superga:
Make your way to the Basilica of Superga, situated on a hill overlooking Turin. Climb to the top and enjoy breathtaking panoramic views of the city and the Alps. Take a moment to explore the basilica's interior and appreciate its architectural beauty.

16. Go Underground at the Turin Undergrounds:

Discover the hidden side of Turin by exploring its underground tunnels and chambers. Take a guided tour of the Turin Undergrounds and learn about the city's fascinating subterranean history.

17. Enjoy Outdoor Activities in the Gran Paradiso National Park:
Nature lovers should venture to the Gran Paradiso National Park, the oldest national park in Italy. Embark on hiking trails, spot wildlife such as ibex and chamois, and relish the tranquility of the pristine alpine environment.

18. Marvel at the Sacro Monte di Crea:
Visit the Sacro Monte di Crea, a hilltop sanctuary with a series of chapels depicting scenes from the life of Saint Francis of Assisi. Take a walk through the park surrounding the sanctuary and enjoy

the panoramic views of the surrounding countryside.

19. Explore the Castle of Racconigi:

Discover the Castle of Racconigi, a stunning royal residence surrounded by beautiful gardens. Explore the castle's interiors, stroll through the park, and admire the ornate architecture and exquisite decorations.

20. Relax in the Thermal Baths of Acqui Terme:

Unwind and rejuvenate in the thermal baths of Acqui Terme. Enjoy the therapeutic properties of the mineral-rich waters, indulge in spa treatments, and experience ultimate relaxation in this charming spa town.

These are just a few of the many incredible things to do in Turin and the

Piedmont region. Whether you're interested in history, art, nature, or gastronomy, this captivating part of Northern Italy offers a myriad of experiences to delight every traveler. Soak in the rich cultural heritage, indulge in delectable cuisine, and create unforgettable memories in Turin and the Piedmont region.

Chapter 5

Emilia-Romagna

Emilia-Romagna, located in the heart of Northern Italy, is a region renowned for its rich cultural heritage, culinary traditions, and beautiful landscapes. With its vibrant cities, charming towns, and fertile countryside, Emilia-Romagna offers a diverse range of experiences that capture the essence of Italian life.

Emilia-Romagna is known for its historical significance, dating back to the time of the Etruscans and Romans. The region is home to several UNESCO World Heritage sites, including the city of Ferrara, with its well-preserved Renaissance architecture and medieval city walls. Bologna, the regional capital, boasts a rich history and is famous for its impressive porticoes, ancient towers, and one of the oldest universities in the world.

Culinary delights are a cornerstone of Emilia-Romagna's identity. The region is often hailed as Italy's food capital, renowned for its Parmigiano Reggiano cheese, traditional balsamic vinegar, and Parma ham. Food enthusiasts can explore the region's culinary trails, visit local producers, and indulge in authentic flavors at trattorias, osterias, and street markets. Bologna's food scene is particularly vibrant, with its famous fresh pasta dishes, such as tortellini and tagliatelle al ragù, drawing visitors from far and wide.

Emilia-Romagna's cities are also cultural hubs, offering a wealth of artistic and architectural treasures. Ravenna, known for its stunning Byzantine mosaics, showcases a unique blend of Roman and Byzantine influences. Modena, birthplace of renowned opera singer Luciano Pavarotti, is home to a magnificent cathedral and the iconic Ferrari Museum, celebrating the region's automotive heritage.

The region's countryside is dotted with picturesque villages and rolling hills, creating a charming backdrop for exploration. The Po River Delta, a UNESCO Biosphere Reserve, offers nature lovers the opportunity to observe diverse bird species and explore tranquil wetlands. The Apennine Mountains provide breathtaking landscapes, ideal for hiking, biking, and skiing in winter.

Emilia-Romagna also boasts a vibrant cultural scene, hosting numerous festivals and events throughout the year. The city of Parma is celebrated for its opera, with its renowned Teatro Regio showcasing world-class performances. The coastal town of Rimini attracts visitors with its lively nightlife, beautiful beaches, and historical attractions.

Motor enthusiasts are drawn to Emilia-Romagna for its deep-rooted connection to the automotive industry. The region is home to iconic car manufacturers. Visitors can explore museums and factories, and even experience thrilling test drives on legendary racing circuits.

In addition to its cultural and culinary offerings, Emilia-Romagna is known for its warm and welcoming spirit. The locals, known as "emiliani" and "romagnoli," take pride in their region's traditions and are eager to share their love for its history, art, and gastronomy with visitors.

Emilia-Romagna truly embodies the essence of Italian charm, offering a harmonious blend of history, culture, and culinary delights. Whether you're exploring its vibrant cities, indulging in its gastronomic treasures, or immersing yourself in its picturesque landscapes, Emilia-Romagna promises an unforgettable journey through the heart of Italy.

Where to Stay

When it comes to finding the perfect place to stay in Emilia-Romagna, you'll be filled for choice. This captivating region in

Northern Italy offers a diverse range of accommodations, from luxurious hotels to charming agriturismos and cozy bed and breakfasts. Whether you're looking for a city escape, a countryside retreat, or a coastal getaway, Emilia-Romagna has something to suit every traveler's taste. Let's explore some of the region's top destinations and recommended places to stay.

1. Bologna:

As the regional capital, Bologna offers a wide selection of accommodations to suit different budgets and preferences. The city center is a popular choice for those who want to be in the heart of the action. Here, you'll find elegant boutique hotels, charming guesthouses, and comfortable apartments within walking distance of the city's main attractions, such as Piazza Maggiore and the historic towers. For a

more tranquil stay, consider the hills surrounding Bologna, where agriturismos and country estates offer a peaceful retreat with panoramic views of the city.
Recommended Hotels in Bologna:

- Grand Hotel Majestic "già Baglioni"
- Art Hotel Commercianti
- Hotel Corona d'Oro

2. Modena:

Modena, known for its rich culinary traditions and UNESCO-listed historic center, offers a range of accommodation options. Stay in the city center to be close to attractions like the Modena Cathedral and the Ghirlandina Tower. You'll find boutique hotels housed in historic buildings, as well as contemporary hotels with modern amenities. If you prefer a more rural setting, consider staying in the countryside outside Modena, where agriturismos and farmhouses offer a peaceful retreat surrounded by vineyards and countryside views.

Recommended Hotels in Modena:

- Hotel Canalgrande
- Hotel Real Fini Baia Del Re
- Hotel Rua Frati

3. **Parma**:

Parma, famous for its prosciutto, Parmigiano Reggiano cheese, and opera heritage, offers a range of accommodations to suit different tastes. Stay in the city center to explore attractions like the Parma Cathedral and the Teatro Regio. Here, you'll find boutique hotels, charming bed and breakfasts, and comfortable apartments. For a more rural experience, consider staying in the nearby countryside, where agriturismos and country estates offer a peaceful atmosphere and the chance to immerse yourself in the region's culinary traditions.

Recommended Hotels in Parma:

- Grand Hotel de La Ville
- Hotel Torino
- Hotel Button

4. Ravenna:

Ravenna, renowned for its Byzantine mosaics and UNESCO World Heritage sites, offers a range of accommodations to suit different preferences. Stay in the city center to be close to attractions like the Basilica of San Vitale and the Mausoleum of Galla Placidia. You'll find boutique hotels, cozy guesthouses, and budget-friendly options within walking distance of the city's historic treasures. If you prefer a more coastal setting, consider staying in one of the beach resorts along the Adriatic coast, just a short drive from Ravenna.

Recommended Hotels in Ravenna:

- Palazzo Bezzi Hotel
- Mosaico Hotel
- NH Ravenna

5. Rimini:

Rimini, a popular coastal destination in Emilia-Romagna, offers a wide range of accommodations along its stunning beaches. Choose from luxurious beachfront resorts with private pools and spa facilities, or opt for budget-friendly hotels and guesthouses just steps away from the sandy shores. Rimini's vibrant nightlife scene and proximity to attractions like the Tempio Malatestiano and the Arch of Augustus make it an ideal base for beach lovers and culture enthusiasts alike.

Recommended Hotels in Rimini:

- Grand Hotel Rimini
- Hotel Aria
- Hotel Sporting
- Hotel Villa Rosa Riviera

6. Ferrara:
Ferrara, with its well-preserved Renaissance architecture and medieval charm, offers a range of accommodations to enhance your stay. Choose to stay in the city center to be within walking distance of attractions like the Estense Castle and the Ferrara Cathedral. Here, you'll find boutique hotels housed in historic buildings, as well as cozy bed and breakfasts with a personal touch. For a more tranquil setting, consider staying in the countryside surrounding Ferrara, where agriturismos and country retreats offer a peaceful escape.

Recommended Hotels in Ferrara:

- Hotel Ferrara
- Hotel Orologio
- Hotel Annunziata

7. <u>Parma Apennines</u>:
The picturesque Parma Apennines, with its breathtaking landscapes and charming villages, provides an ideal setting for those seeking a rural retreat. Stay in the countryside and enjoy the tranquility of the hills, vineyards, and forests. Agriturismos and country houses in this area offer comfortable accommodations, often with on-site restaurants serving traditional regional cuisine. You'll have the opportunity to explore the natural beauty of the region, hike along scenic trails, and indulge in local culinary delights.

Recommended Accommodations in Parma Apennines:

- Locanda Ca' Matilde
- Agriturismo Le Querce
- Locanda Mariella

8. Coastal Towns:
Emilia-Romagna's Adriatic coast is dotted with charming coastal towns and beach resorts, providing a relaxing escape by the sea. Rimini, Cervia, and Cesenatico are popular choices for beach lovers, offering a wide range of accommodations, from luxury resorts to family-friendly hotels. Enjoy direct access to the sandy beaches, sunbathe by the pool, and indulge in fresh seafood at the local restaurants. These coastal towns also offer vibrant nightlife, entertainment options, and a variety of water sports activities.

Recommended Accommodations in Coastal Towns:

- Hotel Waldorf - Rimini
- Hotel Lungomare - Cesenatico
- Hotel Kursaal - Cervia

Emilia-Romagna's diverse landscapes and vibrant cities provide a multitude of options for accommodations, ensuring a comfortable and enjoyable stay. Whether you prefer the cultural immersion of a city center hotel, the tranquility of a countryside retreat, or the relaxation of a beachfront resort, you'll find the perfect place to stay in this captivating region. Embrace the warmth and hospitality of the locals as you embark on a memorable journey through Emilia-Romagna.

What to Eat and Where

When it comes to culinary delights, Emilia-Romagna takes center stage as a gastronomic paradise in Northern Italy. Prepare your taste buds for an extraordinary journey through a region renowned for its rich culinary traditions and delectable dishes. From savory cured meats to creamy cheeses, handmade pastas to flavorful sauces, and heavenly desserts to robust wines, Emilia-Romagna offers a feast for all your senses.

1. **Tagliatelle al Ragù**: Silky ribbons of pasta served with a slow-cooked meat sauce. Try it at **Trattoria Anna Maria** in Bologna for an authentic taste.

2. **Tortellini en Brodo**: Delicate pasta pockets filled with savory fillings, served in a flavorful broth. Visit **Trattoria Serghei**

in Modena for a delightful bowl of tortellini.

3. Lasagna: Layers of homemade pasta, rich ragù, and creamy béchamel sauce. Savour the classic lasagna at **Osteria del Mirasole** in San Giovanni in Persiceto.

4. Parmigiano Reggiano: A renowned aged cheese with a nutty flavor. Visit a local cheese factory in Parma like **Caseificio San Pier Damiani** to witness the production process and taste the best Parmigiano Reggiano.

5. Squacquerone: Creamy and delicate cheese often spread on warm piadina. Enjoy it at **Piadineria La Viga** in Rimini for an authentic experience.

6. Prosciutto di Parma: Dry-cured ham with a delicate balance of saltiness and sweetness. Sample the finest prosciutto at **Prosciutteria Cantina Maestrella** in Parma.

7. Mortadella: Finely ground pork sausage studded with pistachios. Try it at **Salumeria Simoni** in Bologna, where you can find a wide selection of high-quality cured meats.

8. Coppa: Marbled cured pork shoulder with a robust flavor. Visit **Salumeria Bruno e Franco** in Modena for their exceptional coppa.

9. Aceto Balsamico Tradizionale: Traditional balsamic vinegar with a complex and sweet flavor. Explore the ancient cellars of **Acetaia Villa San Donnino** in Modena for an immersive balsamic vinegar experience.

10. **Piadina Romagnola**: Thin, unleavened flatbread often filled with various ingredients. Enjoy a delicious piadina at **La Piadina del Melograno** in Rimini.

Remember, these are just a few highlights of Emilia-Romagna's culinary delights. Exploring local markets, visiting traditional trattorias, and interacting with locals will uncover even more mouthwatering dishes and hidden gems.

Tourist Attractions in Emilia-Romagna

Emilia-Romagna, located in the heart of Italy, is a region that boasts a wealth of captivating tourist attractions. From historic cities to breathtaking landscapes, there's something for every traveler to discover. Here are some of the top attractions in Emilia-Romagna:

1. Bologna: The region's capital, Bologna, is a vibrant city known for its rich history and stunning architecture. Don't miss the iconic *Two Towers* (Due Torri), the historic *University of Bologna*, and the beautiful *Piazza Maggiore*.

2. Ravenna: A UNESCO World Heritage Site, Ravenna is renowned for its exquisite Byzantine mosaics. Explore the stunning mosaics in the Basilica of San Vitale, the Mausoleum of Galla Placidia, and the Basilica of Sant'Apollinare Nuovo.

3. Modena: Famous for its culinary contributions, Modena is a must-visit for food enthusiasts. Explore the stunning *Modena Cathedral*, and savor the traditional balsamic vinegar of the region.

4. Parma: Known for its cultural and culinary heritage, Parma is a city brimming with artistic treasures. Visit the magnificent _Parma Cathedral_, the _Teatro Farnese_, and indulge in the city's renowned Parmigiano Reggiano and prosciutto.

5. Rimini: With its long sandy beaches and lively atmosphere, Rimini is a popular destination for sun-seekers. Take a stroll along the promenade, visit the ancient Roman Arch of Augustus, and explore the historic old town.

6. San Marino: Although not technically part of Emilia-Romagna, San Marino is a small independent state located within its borders. Discover the enchanting mountaintop city-state, explore its medieval fortresses, and enjoy panoramic views of the surrounding landscapes.

7. Cinque Terre: While not within Emilia-Romagna itself, the picturesque coastal villages of Cinque Terre are easily accessible from the region. Take a day trip to these colorful fishing villages and hike along the scenic coastal trails.

8. Po Delta Park: Nature lovers will appreciate the beauty of the Po Delta Park, a vast wetland area teeming with diverse wildlife. Enjoy boat tours, birdwatching, and peaceful walks in this unique natural setting.

These attractions are just a taste of what Emilia-Romagna has to offer. Whether you're drawn to history, art, gastronomy, or natural beauty, this captivating region will leave you with unforgettable memories. Explore, indulge, and immerse yourself in the unique charm of Emilia-Romagna.

Things to do in Emilia-Romagna

Emilia-Romagna is a region of Italy that offers a wide array of activities and experiences for visitors. From cultural treasures to culinary delights, here are some of the top things to do in Emilia-Romagna:

1. **Explore the historic city of Bologna**: Take a stroll through the medieval streets of Bologna, visit the iconic Two Towers, and explore the fascinating historic center, Piazza Maggiore.

2. **Indulge in the culinary delights**: Emilia-Romagna is renowned for its food culture. Treat your taste buds to traditional dishes such as tortellini,

lasagna, prosciutto di Parma, and Parmigiano Reggiano cheese.

3. **Explore the mosaics of Ravenna**: Marvel at the intricate Byzantine mosaics in Ravenna's UNESCO World Heritage sites, including the Basilica of San Vitale and the Mausoleum of Galla Placidia.

4. **Discover the art in Modena**: Visit the stunning Modena Cathedral, a UNESCO World Heritage site, and explore the city's vibrant art scene.

5. **Relax on the Adriatic Coast**: Emilia-Romagna is home to beautiful sandy beaches along the Adriatic Coast. Enjoy sunbathing, swimming, and water sports in popular beach resorts such as Rimini and Riccione.

6. Take a trip to Parma: Explore the charming city of Parma and visit attractions like the Teatro Farnese, Parma Cathedral, and the birthplace of composer Giuseppe Verdi.

7. Enjoy the natural beauty of the Apennine Mountains: Embark on scenic hikes or bike rides in the picturesque Apennine Mountains, which offer breathtaking views and opportunities for outdoor activities.

8. Attend the opera at the Verdi Festival: If you're a fan of opera, don't miss the opportunity to attend the Verdi Festival in Parma, dedicated to the works of renowned composer Giuseppe Verdi.

9. Explore the charming town of Cesenatico: Wander through the picturesque streets and canals of

Cesenatico, known for its historic port and maritime heritage.

10. **Visit the Malatestiana Library in Cesena**: Admire the beauty of the Malatestiana Library, one of the oldest public libraries in Europe, known for its stunning architecture and collection of ancient manuscripts.

11. **Take a wine tour in the hills of Romagna:** Discover the vineyards and wineries of the Romagna region, famous for its Sangiovese wines. Enjoy wine tastings and learn about the winemaking process.

12. **Immerse yourself in the Italian lifestyle**: Emilia-Romagna offers a chance to experience the authentic Italian lifestyle. Enjoy leisurely meals at local

trattorias, explore traditional markets, and interact with friendly locals.

These are just a few of the many things to do and experience in Emilia-Romagna. Whether you're passionate about art, history, food, or nature, this captivating region has something for everyone to enjoy. Immerse yourself in its rich culture and create unforgettable memories during your visit to Emilia-Romagna.

Chapter 6

Discovering Friuli-Venezia Giulia

Friuli-Venezia Giulia, nestled in the northeastern corner of Italy, is a captivating region that seamlessly blends cultural diversity, stunning landscapes, and a rich historical heritage. From the peaks of the Julian Alps to the azure waters of the Adriatic Sea, Friuli-Venezia Giulia offers a unique and unforgettable experience for visitors. Let's embark on a perfect overview of this enchanting region.

Friuli-Venezia Giulia is a land of contrasts, characterized by its diverse cultural influences. It borders Austria and

Slovenia, which have left a significant mark on the region's history, traditions, and architecture. This cultural fusion is reflected in the charming towns and villages, where Italian, Austrian, and Slavic influences converge to create a distinctive atmosphere.

The region's capital, _Trieste_, is a captivating city that showcases its historical grandeur and maritime heritage. The elegant Piazza Unità d'Italia, overlooking the Adriatic Sea, serves as a focal point for the city's bustling atmosphere. Explore the narrow streets of the Old Town, visit the magnificent Miramare Castle, and indulge in the city's renowned coffee culture.

Nature enthusiasts will be enthralled by the diverse landscapes of Friuli-Venezia Giulia. The Julian Alps offer breathtaking mountain vistas, pristine lakes, and hiking trails that cater to all levels of experience. The stunning Dolomites, a UNESCO World Heritage site, beckon adventure seekers with their jagged peaks and scenic beauty.

For wine enthusiasts, Friuli-Venezia Giulia is a paradise. The region is renowned for its exceptional wines, including Friulano, Ribolla Gialla, and Refosco. Explore the picturesque vineyards of the Collio and Colli Orientali del Friuli wine regions, taste exquisite wines in family-run wineries, and savor the local gastronomic delights that perfectly complement the wines.

The region's gastronomy is a reflection of its diverse cultural influences. Friuli-Venezia Giulia boasts a rich culinary tradition that combines Italian, Austrian, and Slavic flavors. Indulge in hearty dishes such as frico (a cheese and potato pancake), jota (a bean and sauerkraut soup), and delicious seafood specialties along the Adriatic coast.

Historical and architectural wonders are also abundant in Friuli-Venezia Giulia. Visit the town of Aquileia, an ancient Roman city that boasts impressive archaeological ruins and a stunning basilica. Explore the medieval town of Cividale del Friuli, with its Lombard Temple and Ponte del Diavolo (Devil's Bridge), both UNESCO World Heritage sites.

Friuli-Venezia Giulia's proximity to the Adriatic Sea offers visitors a chance to unwind on its beautiful sandy beaches, particularly in popular resort towns such as Grado and Lignano Sabbiadoro. The region's coastline is dotted with charming fishing villages, where you can savor freshly caught seafood and enjoy leisurely walks along the promenades.

The region also hosts a variety of cultural events and festivals throughout the year, celebrating its diverse heritage. From music and film festivals to traditional folkloric events, there is always something to discover and experience in Friuli-Venezia Giulia.

Friuli-Venezia Giulia captivates visitors with its natural beauty, cultural diversity, and warm hospitality. If you're seeking outdoor adventures, culinary delights, historical treasures, or a blend of all three, this remarkable region offers a unique and immersive experience that will leave a lasting impression. Immerse yourself in the enchanting atmosphere of

Friuli-Venezia Giulia and discover the hidden gems that await you at every turn.

Where to Stay

When it comes to finding the perfect place to stay in Friuli-Venezia Giulia, you'll be delighted by the range of options available. From charming hotels in historic towns to picturesque countryside retreats and coastal resorts, the region offers a diverse selection of accommodations to suit every traveler's preferences. Let's explore some recommended places to stay in Friuli-Venezia Giulia.

1. Trieste:

As the regional capital, Trieste offers a wide range of accommodations to choose from. Stay in the heart of the city near Piazza Unità d'Italia for easy access to the main attractions, including the historic center and waterfront. You'll find elegant hotels with stunning sea views, boutique guesthouses tucked away in charming side streets, and modern apartments for a more independent stay. Consider accommodations in the historic districts of Città Vecchia or Cavana for a truly immersive experience.

Recommended Hotels in Trieste:

- Savoia Excelsior Palace
- Hotel Continentale
- Hotel Victoria Trieste

2. **Udine**:

Udine, known for its elegant architecture and vibrant atmosphere, offers a range of accommodations in and around the city center. Stay in the historic center to be close to attractions like Piazza della Libertà and the Venetian Loggia. Choose from boutique hotels housed in historic buildings, modern hotels with stylish amenities, or cozy bed and breakfasts for a more intimate stay. For a peaceful escape, consider accommodations in the nearby countryside, where agriturismos and country estates provide a tranquil retreat.

<u>Recommended Hotels in Udine</u>:

- Hotel Friuli
- Astoria Hotel Italia
- Hotel Suite Inn

<u>3. Gorizia</u>:

Gorizia, a charming town near the border with Slovenia, offers a selection of accommodations to suit different preferences. Stay in the town center to explore attractions like the Castle of Gorizia and the Piazza della Transalpina. You'll find hotels with a mix of modern and traditional features, as well as family-run guesthouses with a personal touch. For a more rural experience, consider accommodations in the surrounding countryside, where agriturismos and farm stays offer a peaceful retreat.

Recommended Hotels in Gorizia:

- Best Western Gorizia Palace Hotel
- Grand Hotel Entourage
- Hotel Internazionale Gorizia

4. **Grado**:

Grado, a popular seaside resort on the Adriatic coast, offers a range of accommodations for beach lovers. Stay in one of the beachfront hotels or resorts to enjoy direct access to the sandy shores and panoramic sea views. You'll find accommodations with swimming pools, spa facilities, and restaurants serving delicious seafood specialties. For a more intimate experience, consider staying in a bed and breakfast or an apartment within walking distance of the beach.

Recommended Hotels in Grado:

- Laguna Palace Hotel
- Grand Hotel Astoria
- Hotel Hannover

5. Cividale del Friuli:

Cividale del Friuli, a UNESCO World Heritage site, is a charming medieval town with a rich history and beautiful architecture. Stay in the town center to explore attractions such as the Lombard Temple and the Devil's Bridge. You'll find boutique hotels and guesthouses that offer a blend of comfort and historical charm. Enjoy the town's vibrant atmosphere, stroll along the picturesque streets, and immerse yourself in its cultural heritage.

Recommended Hotels in Cividale del Friuli:

- Palazzo Scolari
- Hotel Roma
- Locanda al Castello

6. Sauris:

Sauris is a picturesque mountain village nestled in the Carnic Alps, known for its traditional wooden houses and stunning alpine scenery. Stay in one of the local guesthouses or mountain lodges for an authentic experience. Enjoy the tranquility of the surroundings, go hiking or skiing in the nearby mountains, and savor the local smoked ham and cheese that the village is famous for.

Recommended Accommodations in Sauris:

- Albergo Diffuso Sauris
- Gasthof Sauris
- Hotel La Perla

7. Trieste Karst:
The Trieste Karst, with its unique landscape of karst formations and underground caves, offers a distinctive accommodation experience. Stay in one of the charming agriturismos or rural guest houses located amidst vineyards and olive groves. Immerse yourself in the peaceful countryside, explore the karst caves, and indulge in local wines and traditional cuisine.

Recommended Accommodations in the Trieste Karst:

- Agriturismo Kovač
- Albergo Ristorante Belvedere
- Agriturismo Terra et Volta

Friuli-Venezia Giulia provides a variety of accommodation options to cater to different preferences and budgets. Whether you prefer the vibrant city atmosphere, the tranquility of the countryside, or the seaside charm, you'll find the perfect place to stay in this captivating region. Immerse yourself in the unique ambiance of Friuli-Venezia Giulia and enjoy a memorable stay that combines comfort, hospitality, and the region's distinctive character.

What to Eat and Where

Friuli-Venezia Giulia, located in northeastern Italy, is known for its unique culinary heritage that combines Italian, Austrian, and Slovenian influences. Here are some delicious dishes to try and recommended places to indulge in them while exploring Friuli-Venezia Giulia:

1. Prosciutto di San Daniele: Sample the world-renowned cured ham from **San Daniele del Friuli**. Visit a local prosciutto factory or enjoy it at traditional trattorias and osterias.

2. Gubana: This traditional pastry from the town of Gorizia is a sweet delight. It features a spiral of dough filled with a mixture of dried fruits, nuts, and spices. Look for it in local bakeries.

3. Frico: This popular Friulian dish is a savory cheese and potato pancake. It is often made with Montasio cheese and can be found in many traditional taverns and agriturismi (farm stays).

4. Brovada con Musèt: A traditional dish from the city of Udine, it consists of pickled turnips (brovada) served with boiled pork sausage (musèt). Enjoy it at local osterias and trattorias.

5. <u>Jota</u>: This hearty bean and sauerkraut soup is a staple of Friulian cuisine. It is often flavored with smoked meats such as pancetta or sausage. Taste it at rustic trattorias and agriturismi.

6. <u>Frico Friulano</u>: Another variation of frico, this dish consists of a crispy cheese and potato pancake. It is a delicious specialty found in mountainous areas and traditional alpine huts.

7. <u>Sclopit</u>: This traditional fish stew is a specialty of the coastal towns in Friuli-Venezia Giulia. It typically includes a variety of fish and shellfish simmered in a flavorful tomato broth. Enjoy it at seaside restaurants.

8. Fasòt: These slow-cooked beans are a regional specialty often served with polenta. Look for it in traditional restaurants and agriturismi.

9. Canederli: Also known as "gnocchi alla trentina," these bread dumplings are a regional favorite. They are usually served in a hearty broth or with melted butter and cheese. Find them in cozy mountain taverns.

10. Cjalsons: These stuffed pasta pockets are a unique delicacy of the Carnia region. They are filled with a mixture of sweet and savory ingredients such as herbs, cheese, and dried fruit. Taste them at local festivals or traditional eateries.

When exploring Friuli-Venezia Giulia, it's recommended to visit local trattorias, osterias, and agriturismi to savor the regional cuisine. Each town and village will have its own specialties and local dishes to discover. Don't hesitate to ask the locals for their recommendations, as they will often point you to the best places to experience the authentic flavors of Friuli-Venezia Giulia.

Top Attractions in Friuli-Venezia Giulia

Friuli-Venezia Giulia offers a diverse range of attractions that blend natural beauty, historical sites, and cultural experiences. Here are some of the top attractions to visit in Friuli-Venezia Giulia:

1. **Trieste**: Explore the charming city of Trieste, known for its rich history, elegant architecture, and stunning coastal views. Visit the *Piazza Unità d'Italia, Miramare*

Castle, and the impressive _Trieste Cathedral_.

2. Aquileia: Discover the ancient Roman city of Aquileia, a UNESCO World Heritage site. Explore the fascinating archaeological area, including the Basilica di Aquileia with its stunning mosaics.

3. Castello di Miramare: Admire the beautiful Miramare Castle, located on the Gulf of Trieste. Explore the opulent interiors, stroll through the picturesque gardens, and enjoy breathtaking views of the Adriatic Sea.

4. Cividale del Friuli: Visit the historic town of Cividale del Friuli, known for its Lombard heritage. Explore the charming old town, see the iconic Ponte del Diavolo (Devil's Bridge), and visit the Tempietto

Longobardo, a UNESCO World Heritage site.

5. Gorizia: Experience the unique blend of Italian and Slovenian influences in the border town of Gorizia. Visit the Castle of Gorizia, stroll through the historic center, and enjoy panoramic views from the Gorizia Hill.

6. Grotta Gigante: Venture into the Grotta Gigante, one of the largest tourist caves in the world. Marvel at its enormous chambers, stalactites, and stalagmites during a guided tour.

7. Palmanova: Explore the remarkable star-shaped fortress town of Palmanova. Take a walk along its impressive ramparts, visit the Cathedral of Sant'Agnese, and soak in the historical atmosphere.

8. Prosecco Hills: Discover the scenic Prosecco Hills, renowned for their vineyards and wine production. Take a tour of the wineries, enjoy tastings of the famous Prosecco sparkling wine, and savor the picturesque landscapes.

9. Sauris: Visit the picturesque village of Sauris, nestled in the Carnic Alps. Explore its charming wooden houses, taste the local smoked ham, and enjoy outdoor activities such as hiking and skiing.

10. Duino Castle: Marvel at the majestic Duino Castle, perched on a cliff overlooking the Adriatic Sea. Explore its elegant rooms, stroll through the gardens, and enjoy panoramic views from the tower.

11. Grado: Relax in the seaside town of Grado, known for its sandy beaches and therapeutic thermal spas. Enjoy sunbathing, swimming, and exploring the historic center with its Byzantine heritage.

12. San Daniele del Friuli: Indulge in the famous San Daniele prosciutto in the charming town of San Daniele del Friuli. Visit the prosciutto factories, learn about the production process, and sample this exquisite cured ham.

13. Tarvisio: Experience the beauty of the Julian Alps in the town of Tarvisio. Enjoy outdoor activities like hiking, skiing, and mountain biking, and admire the stunning natural landscapes.

14. Udine: Immerse yourself in the artistic and cultural heritage of Udine. Explore the historic center with its Renaissance architecture, visit the Castle of Udine, and appreciate the vibrant local art scene.

15. Friulian Dolomites: Discover the stunning landscapes of the Friulian Dolomites. Embark on hikes or scenic drives, admire the rugged peaks and pristine alpine lakes, and enjoy the tranquility of nature.

Whether you're drawn to history, nature, or cultural experiences, Friuli-Venezia Giulia has something to offer every traveler. Explore its diverse attractions, immerse yourself in its rich heritage, and savor the unique blend of Italian, Austrian, and Slovenian influences that make this region truly captivating.

Things to do in Friuli-Venezia Giulia

Friuli-Venezia Giulia is a captivating region in northeastern Italy, known for its rich history, stunning landscapes, and cultural diversity. Here are some top things to do and experiences to enjoy in Friuli-Venezia Giulia:

1. Visit Trieste: Begin your exploration in the charming city of Trieste, known for its beautiful architecture, historic cafes, and maritime heritage. Explore the *Piazza Unità d'Italia,* the largest sea-facing square in Europe, and visit attractions like the *Trieste Cathedral and Miramare Castle.*

2. Discover the Castello di Miramare: Situated on a rocky promontory overlooking the Adriatic Sea, Miramare Castle is a must-visit. Explore the beautifully preserved interiors, stroll through the enchanting gardens, and enjoy breathtaking views of the coastline.

3. **Explore the Grotta Gigante**: Embark on an underground adventure in the Grotta Gigante, one of the world's largest tourist caves. Marvel at the impressive stalactite and stalagmite formations as you explore the illuminated pathways.

4. **Taste the Wine of Collio:** Friuli-Venezia Giulia is renowned for its exceptional wines, particularly those produced in the Collio region. Take a wine tour, visit local vineyards, and savor the exquisite flavors of Friulian wines, including the famous white wines.

5. **Discover Aquileia's Roman Ruins**: Step back in time and explore the ancient Roman city of Aquileia, a UNESCO World

Heritage Site. Marvel at the well-preserved ruins, including the ancient forum, basilica, and mosaic floors.

6. **Relax at the Beaches of Grado**: Escape to the beautiful seaside town of Grado and enjoy its golden sandy beaches. Take a dip in the clear waters of the Adriatic Sea, unwind at beachfront cafes, and explore the historic center with its narrow streets and charming squares.

7. **Experience the Carnia Region**: Venture into the picturesque Carnia region, known for its pristine nature and traditional mountain villages. Go hiking in the Carnic Alps, visit historic churches and chapels, and immerse yourself in the local culture.

8. **Visit the Duino Castle**: Discover the enchanting Duino Castle, perched on a cliff overlooking the Gulf of Trieste.

Explore its magnificent halls, stroll through the beautiful gardens, and enjoy panoramic views of the Adriatic coastline.

9. Explore the Julian Alps: For outdoor enthusiasts, the Julian Alps offer a plethora of activities. Go hiking, climbing, or mountain biking in the breathtaking natural landscapes, and enjoy the fresh mountain air and stunning vistas.

10. Attend the Festa della Transumanza: Experience the traditional Festa della Transumanza, a celebration of the seasonal migration of livestock from the mountains to the plains. Witness colorful parades, cultural performances, and local traditions.

11. Enjoy Water Sports in Lignano Sabbiadoro: Head to the lively beach resort town of Lignano Sabbiadoro and indulge in a variety of water sports. Try your hand at windsurfing, sailing, or paddleboarding, or simply relax on the sandy beaches.

12. Explore the Cividale del Friuli: Visit the charming town of Cividale del Friuli, with its medieval architecture and historic center. Admire the stunning Lombard Temple, stroll along the Ponte del Diavolo (Devil's Bridge), and visit the National Archaeological Museum.

13. Explore the Miramare Marine Nature Reserve: Discover the underwater wonders of the Miramare Marine Nature Reserve, located along the coast near Trieste. Take a snorkeling or diving excursion to witness the rich marine life and vibrant coral reefs.

14. Visit the Prosciutto Village of San Daniele: Journey to the charming village of San Daniele, renowned for its production of prosciutto (cured ham). Take a tour of a prosciutto factory, learn about the traditional curing process, and indulge in a tasting of this delicious delicacy.

15. Discover the Castle of Udine: Explore the Castle of Udine, a magnificent fortress that dominates the city's skyline. Visit the castle museum to learn about the region's history and admire the panoramic views from the tower.

Chapter 7

Italian Lakes and Alpine Retreats

Situated in the beautiful landscape of Northern Italy, the Italian Lakes and Alpine region offer a breathtaking combination of stunning lakes, majestic mountains, and charming towns. This picturesque area is renowned for its natural beauty, outdoor activities, and idyllic lakeside retreats. Let's delve into an enchanting overview of the Italian Lakes and Alpine region.

The Italian Lakes are a collection of serene bodies of water that captivate visitors with their crystal-clear depths, surrounded by lush greenery and towering mountains. The most famous lakes include **Lake Como, Lake Garda, Lake Maggiore, Lake Orta, and Lake Lugano.** Each lake has its own unique character, yet all share a common allure that draws travelers seeking tranquility and natural splendor.

Lake Como, often described as the jewel of the Italian Lakes, is known for its enchanting villas, charming towns, and stunning vistas. Explore the picturesque town of Bellagio, with its cobbled streets and elegant villas. Take a boat ride on the lake, marvel at the opulent gardens of Villa Carlotta, and soak in the breathtaking views of the surrounding mountains.

Lake Garda, the largest lake in Italy, offers a perfect blend of natural beauty and recreational activities. The picturesque towns of Sirmione, Malcesine, and Riva del Garda are popular destinations, offering historic sites, waterfront promenades, and watersports opportunities. Explore the ancient Scaliger Castle, take a cable car ride to Mount Baldo for panoramic views, or simply relax on the lake's shores and enjoy the serene atmosphere.

Lake Maggiore, shared between Italy and Switzerland, is known for its charming islands, such as Isola Bella and Isola dei Pescatori. Visit the grand Borromeo Palace on Isola Bella, with its exquisite gardens and ornate interiors. Explore the quaint streets of Stresa, a charming lakeside town, or take a scenic boat tour to admire the captivating landscapes that surround the lake.

Lake Orta, often referred to as a hidden gem, offers a peaceful retreat away from the crowds. Discover the idyllic town of Orta San Giulio, with its narrow streets, medieval buildings, and a captivating island housing the Sacro Monte. Take a leisurely stroll along the lakeside promenade, savor the local cuisine in waterfront restaurants, and soak in the tranquility of this lesser-known lake.

Lake Lugano, located on the border between Italy and Switzerland, combines natural beauty with a touch of cosmopolitan charm. Explore the city of Lugano, with its elegant shops, art galleries, and vibrant café culture. Take a boat ride on the lake, hike through the surrounding mountains, or simply relax and enjoy the serene atmosphere of this enchanting destination.

The Alpine region, with its majestic peaks and breathtaking landscapes, offers a paradise for outdoor enthusiasts and nature lovers. The Italian Alps are a playground for hiking, skiing, and mountaineering. Explore the stunning Dolomites, a UNESCO World Heritage site, with its towering peaks, dramatic cliffs, and picturesque valleys. Discover the Aosta Valley, with its charming alpine villages, medieval castles, and access to iconic peaks like <u>Monte Cervino</u> (Matterhorn) and <u>Mont Blanc</u>.

The Italian Lakes and Alpine region not only offer stunning natural beauty but also boast a rich cultural heritage. Explore charming lakeside towns, visit historic castles and palaces, indulge in exquisite cuisine, and immerse yourself in the warm hospitality of the locals. Whether you seek adventure in the mountains or serenity by the lakeshores, the Italian Lakes and Alpine region will leave you enchanted and longing to return to its captivating landscapes and idyllic ambiance.

Chapter 8

Transportation Options

When planning a trip to Northern Italy, it's essential to consider the various transportation options available to explore this beautiful region. With its rich history, stunning landscapes, and vibrant cities, Northern Italy offers a multitude of transportation choices to suit every traveler's needs. Whether you prefer the convenience of public transportation or the freedom of a rental car, here is a comprehensive guide to the transportation options in Northern Italy.

1. Air Travel: Northern Italy is well-served by several international airports, making air travel a convenient option for travelers coming from different parts of the world. The main airports in the region include <u>Milan Malpensa Airport</u>, <u>Milan Linate Airport</u>, and <u>Venice Marco Polo Airport</u>. These airports have numerous domestic and international flights, connecting Northern Italy to major cities around the globe. From the airports, you can easily access the region's cities and attractions by using the following transportation options.

2. Train Travel: Trains are an excellent way to explore Northern Italy, offering comfort, convenience, and a scenic journey through the picturesque countryside. The region has an extensive rail network, connecting major cities like Milan, Venice, Verona, Bologna, and Turin. The Italian train system, operated by Trenitalia and Italo, provides frequent and efficient services, including high-speed trains like the _Frecciarossa, Frecciargento,_ and _Frecciabianca._ These trains offer quick connections between cities and are a popular choice for both domestic and international travelers.

3. Public Buses: Public buses are an affordable and reliable means of transportation in Northern Italy, particularly for traveling to smaller towns and rural areas. Local and regional bus services are operated by various companies, such as _ATAC, ACTV, and TPER._ These buses provide connections to remote areas, offering the opportunity to explore off-the-beaten-path destinations and enjoy the scenic beauty of the region. Bus tickets can be purchased at the ticket counters or on board, and it's advisable to check the schedules in advance for a smooth journey.

4. Rental Cars: Renting a car is a popular option for travelers who prefer flexibility and independence during their trip to Northern Italy. Having a car allows you to explore remote areas, visit charming villages, and venture into the countryside at your own pace. Major international car rental companies have offices at the airports and city centers, offering a wide range of vehicles to suit different budgets and preferences. It's important to note that driving in busy city centers can be challenging, and some cities have restricted traffic zones (ZTL) that require permits or are off-limits to non-resident vehicles. Therefore, it's advisable to familiarize yourself with the local driving rules and regulations before embarking on a road trip.

5. **Metro Systems**: Major cities in Northern Italy, such as Milan, Turin, and Bologna, have efficient metro systems that provide convenient transportation within the city. Milan's metro system, known as the _Metropolitana_, has four lines that cover the city center and extend to the outskirts. Turin has a modern metro system with three lines, while Bologna's metro system, known as the Metropolitana di Bologna, connects the city center with the surrounding areas. These metro systems are easy to navigate and offer a quick way to reach popular attractions, shopping districts, and business centers.

6. **Trams and Light Rail**: Trams and light rail systems are prevalent in many cities across Northern Italy, offering an efficient mode of transportation within urban areas. Cities like Milan, Turin, and

Florence have extensive tram networks that complement the metro systems and provide convenient access to different neighborhoods. Trams are an excellent way to explore the city's landmarks, hop-on-hop-off at various attractions, and experience the local culture.

7. Ferries and Boats: Northern Italy is known for its stunning lakes, including Lake Como, Lake Garda, and Lake Maggiore. To fully experience the beauty of these lakes, ferry services and boat tours are available. You can hop on a ferry or cruise boat to explore the picturesque towns and villages nestled along the shores, admire the scenic landscapes, and visit the charming islands. These water transport options provide a unique perspective and offer a relaxing way to enjoy the lakeside scenery.

8. Cycling: Northern Italy is a cyclist's paradise, with its rolling hills, picturesque countryside, and well-developed cycling infrastructure. Many cities, including Milan and Turin, have dedicated cycling lanes and bike-sharing programs, making it easy to explore the urban areas on two wheels. For those seeking a more immersive cycling experience, the region offers numerous cycling routes and trails, such as the famous Via Francigena, which stretches from the Alps to Rome. Renting a bicycle or joining a guided cycling tour allows you to discover the region's natural beauty at a leisurely pace.

9. Taxis and Ridesharing: Taxis are widely available in Northern Italy, particularly in urban areas and near transportation hubs. Official taxis are metered and usually have a fixed starting fee. It's advisable to use licensed taxis and ask for an estimate of the fare before starting your journey. In addition to traditional taxis, ridesharing services like Uber and Lyft operate in some cities, providing an alternative transportation option with upfront pricing and convenient app-based booking.

10. Walking: Exploring Northern Italy on foot is a delightful way to immerse yourself in the local culture, discover hidden gems, and soak in the charming ambiance of the cities and towns. Many cities have well-preserved historic centers, such as Milan's Quadrilatero d'Oro (Golden Quadrilateral) and Venice's labyrinthine streets, which are best explored on foot. Walking tours are also available in various cities, led by knowledgeable guides who provide insights into the history, architecture, and culture of the region.

11. Ski Resorts: Northern Italy is home to several renowned ski resorts, making it a popular destination for winter sports enthusiasts. To reach these resorts, you can use a combination of transportation options, including trains, buses, and private shuttles. The region's proximity to the Alps provides easy access to world-class ski areas such as *Cortina d'Ampezzo*, *Courmayeur*, and *Livigno*. Ski resort transportation services often operate during the winter season, offering convenient transfers between airports, train stations, and the ski resorts themselves.

12. Travel Apps and Online Resources: When navigating the transportation options in Northern Italy, travel apps and online resources can be invaluable tools. There are several apps available, such as

Moovit, and _Citymapper_, which provide real-time information on public transportation routes, schedules, and nearby stops. These apps can help you plan your journey, find the most convenient connections, and stay updated on any disruptions or delays. Additionally, official tourism websites and transportation authority websites provide detailed information on routes, timetables, fares, and special offers, allowing you to make informed decisions about your travel plans.

13. Tips for Efficient Travel: To make the most of your transportation experience in Northern Italy, here are a few additional tips:

- **Plan Ahead**: Research the transportation options available in the specific cities or regions you plan to visit. Check schedules, ticket prices, and any special requirements, such as reservation policies for high-speed trains or restricted traffic zones in city centers.

- **Validate Tickets**: If you are using public transportation, ensure that you validate your ticket before boarding buses or entering metro stations. Failure to validate a ticket may result in fines if checked by ticket inspectors.

- **Consider Peak Hours**: Be mindful of peak hours when using public transportation in major cities. Rush hours in the morning and late afternoon can be crowded, especially on trains and metro systems. If possible, plan your travel outside these peak periods to avoid overcrowding.

- **Purchase Tickets in Advance**: For popular attractions or long-distance train journeys, consider purchasing tickets in advance to secure your seat and potentially benefit from discounted fares. Some attractions offer combined ticket options that include transportation, saving you time and money.

- **Be Aware of Pickpockets**: As with any travel destination, it's important to be vigilant and keep an eye on your belongings, especially in crowded areas or on public transportation. Keep your valuables secure and be cautious of pickpockets.

- ***Learn Basic Italian Phrases***: While many people in Northern Italy speak English, learning a few basic Italian phrases can go a long way in communicating with locals and seeking assistance if needed.

By considering these transportation options and tips, you can navigate Northern Italy with ease, exploring its diverse landscapes, historic sites, and vibrant cities. Whether you choose the convenience of public transportation or the flexibility of a rental car, the region's transportation network ensures that you can enjoy all that Northern Italy has to offer.

Chapter 9

Basic Italian Phrases

In this chapter we're going to embark on a linguistic journey to Italy and explore some essential Italian phrases that will make your travels even more memorable. From greetings to ordering food and asking for directions, we'll cover it all. And don't worry about pronunciation—I'll guide you through it step by step. So, let's dive in!

Greeting and Polite Expressions:
Let's start with greetings and polite expressions, the building blocks of any conversation. Italians are warm and welcoming, so it's essential to greet them

with a smile. Here are a few phrases to get you started:

- **Ciao!** (Hello/Hi!) - Pronunciation: "chow"

Use this informal greeting to say hello to friends, family, or people of your age group.

- **Buongiorno!** (Good morning/Good day!) - Pronunciation: "bwon-jor-no"

This is a general greeting used until late afternoon to greet anyone politely.

- **Buonasera!** (Good evening!) - Pronunciation: "bwon-a-seh-ra"

Use this greeting in the late afternoon and evening to wish someone a good evening.

- **Buonanotte!** (Good night!) - Pronunciation: "bwon-a-not-teh"

This phrase is used to say goodnight or bid farewell in the evening.

- **Grazie!** (Thank you!) - Pronunciation: "gra-tsee-eh"

Express your gratitude with this essential word when someone helps you or offers something.

- **Prego!** (You're welcome/Please) - Pronunciation: "preh-go"

This versatile word can mean "you're welcome" as a response to thank you or "please" when offering something.

Basic Conversational Phrases:

Now, let's learn some phrases that will help you initiate and maintain conversations during your Italian adventures:

- **Come stai?** (How are you?) - Pronunciation: "co-meh stai"

Use this phrase to ask someone how they are feeling or to inquire about their well-being.

- **Scusa/Scusi**. (Excuse me/Sorry.) - Pronunciation: "skoo-zah/skoo-zee"

These words are handy when you want to get someone's attention or apologize for any inconvenience.

- **Parli inglese?** (Do you speak English?) - Pronunciation: "par-lee een-gleh-zeh"

If you find yourself in need of English assistance, this phrase will come in handy.

- **Non capisco**. (I don't understand.) - Pronunciation: "non ka-pee-skoh"

Use this phrase when you need someone to repeat or explain something because you don't understand.

- **Mi scusi, può ripetere per favore?** (Excuse me, can you repeat that please?) - Pronunciation: "mee skoo-zee, pwo ree-peh-teh-reh pehr fa-vo-reh"

This polite request will help you ask someone to repeat what they just said.

Ordering Food and Drinks:

Italian cuisine is renowned worldwide, so let's equip ourselves with some essential phrases for ordering food and drinks:

- **Vorrei...** (I would like...) - Pronunciation: "vo-rray"

Begin your order with this phrase followed by the food or drink item you desire.

- **Un cappuccino, per favore**. (A cappuccino, per favore. (A cappuccino, please.) - Pronunciation: "oon cap-poo-chino, pair fa-vo-reh"

When you're at a café, use this phrase to order a classic Italian cappuccino.

- **Mi può consigliare un piatto tipico?** (Can you recommend a typical dish?)

- Pronunciation: "mee poo kon-seel-yah-reh oon pee-at-toh tee-pee-co"

If you're looking for a local specialty, ask for recommendations with this phrase.

- **Il conto, per favore.** (The bill, please.) - Pronunciation: "eel kohn-toh, pair fa-vo-reh"

When you're ready to settle the bill, politely request it with this phrase.

Asking for Directions:

Exploring a new city often involves navigating unfamiliar streets. Here are some phrases to help you ask for directions:

- **Mi scusi, dov'è...?** (Excuse me, where is...?) - Pronunciation: "mee skoo-zee, doh-veh"

Use this phrase to politely ask for directions to a specific location.

- **A destra/sinistra**. (To the right/left.) - Pronunciation: "ah deh-strah/se-nee-strah"

These words are handy for understanding directions involving right or left turns.

- **Dritto.** (Straight ahead.) - Pronunciation: "dree-toh"

If someone tells you to continue straight, this word will guide your way.

- **Fino a quando arrivo a...?** (How do I get to...?) - Pronunciation: "fee-no ah kwahn-doh ar-ree-voh ah"

When you're unsure about reaching a specific destination, use this phrase to seek guidance.

Emergency Situations:

While we hope you never encounter an emergency, it's crucial to know a few phrases for such situations:

- **Aiuto!** (Help!) - Pronunciation: "ah-yoo-toh"

In case of an emergency, use this word to call for assistance.

- **Chiamate un'ambulanza/polizia.** (Call an ambulance/police.) - Pronunciation: "kee-ah-mah-teh oon-am-boo-lan-tsa/po-lee-tsee-ah"

If you require medical or police assistance, use these phrases to seek help.

- **Ho bisogno di un medico**. (I need a doctor.) - Pronunciation: "oh bee-zoh-nyoh dee oon meh-dee-coh"

If you're in need of medical attention, communicate your situation with this phrase.

Farewells:

As your Italian adventure comes to an end, bid farewell with these phrases:

- **Arrivederci!** (Goodbye!) - Pronunciation: "ar-ree-veh-dehr-chee"

Use this common phrase to say goodbye when parting ways with someone.

- **A presto!** (See you soon!) - Pronunciation: "ah preh-stoh"

If you're optimistic about meeting again, use this phrase to express your intention.

Congratulations! You've now learned some essential Italian phrases that will make your journey through Italy more enjoyable. Remember, practice is key, so don't hesitate to use these phrases with locals. Your effort to communicate in Italian will be greatly appreciated, and it will open doors to deeper cultural connections. Buon viaggio! (Have a good trip!)

Conclusion

As we come to the end of our journey through Northern Italy, I hope this travel guide has provided you with valuable insights, inspiration, and practical information to make your visit truly memorable. Northern Italy is a treasure trove of rich history, breathtaking landscapes, captivating cities, and delectable cuisine. From the bustling streets of Milan to the romantic canals of Venice, the charming beauty of Verona, the cultural richness of Turin, and the hidden gems of Emilia-Romagna, Friuli-Venezia Giulia, and the Italian Lakes region, this diverse region offers something for every traveler.

We have explored the fascinating cities, indulged in authentic Italian cuisine, discovered remarkable attractions, and engaged in vibrant cultural experiences. Whether you are an art enthusiast, a history buff, a food lover, or an adventurer seeking outdoor thrills, Northern Italy has it all.

But beyond the famous landmarks and renowned destinations, what truly makes Northern Italy special is its people—the warm, welcoming Italians who take pride in their heritage and are eager to share their traditions and stories with visitors. It is through these interactions that we gain a deeper understanding of the region's soul and create lasting memories.

As you navigate the streets, savor the flavors, and immerse yourself in the local culture, remember to embrace the Italian way of life—take your time, enjoy leisurely meals, savor every sip of espresso, and indulge in dolce far niente, the sweetness of doing nothing.

While this guide has provided a comprehensive overview, it is merely a starting point for your own unique adventure. Allow yourself to wander off the beaten path, discover hidden gems, and create your own unforgettable experiences.

As you bid farewell to Northern Italy, carry with you the memories of cobblestone streets, enchanting canals, picturesque vineyards, and the warm smiles of the locals. May the spirit of Italy stay with you long after you leave, inspiring you to explore new horizons and embrace the beauty of our diverse world.

Thank you for joining me on this journey, and may your future travels be filled with extraordinary moments and remarkable discoveries. Arrivederci e buon viaggio! (Goodbye and safe travels!)

Made in United States
Troutdale, OR
08/22/2023